21世纪旅游英语系列教材

旅游英语视听说

（第二版）

English for Travel
Audio-visual and Speaking

(Second Edition)

主　编：朱　华
编　者：王雪霏　王　忠

图书在版编目(CIP)数据

旅游英语视听说/朱华主编.—2版.—北京：北京大学出版社，2020.8
21世纪旅游英语系列教材
ISBN 978-7-301-31440-1

Ⅰ.①旅…　Ⅱ.①朱…　Ⅲ.①旅游－英语－听说教学－高等职业教育－教材　Ⅳ.①F59

中国版本图书馆CIP数据核字（2020）第119752号

书　　　名	旅游英语视听说（第二版）
	LÜYOU YINGYU SHI TING SHUO（DI-ER BAN）
著作责任者	朱　华　主编
责任编辑	李　颖
标准书号	ISBN 978-7-301-31440-1
出版发行	北京大学出版社
地　　　址	北京市海淀区成府路205号　100871
网　　　址	http://www.pup.cn　新浪微博：@北京大学出版社
电子信箱	evalee1770@sina.com
电　　　话	邮购部 010-62752015　发行部 010-62750672　编辑部 010-62754382
印刷者	大厂回族自治县彩虹印刷有限公司
经销者	新华书店
	787毫米×1092毫米　16开本　9.25印张　453千字
	2011年1月第1版
	2020年8月第2版　2023年8月第6次印刷
定　　　价	38.00元

未经许可，不得以任何方式复制或抄袭本书之部分或全部内容。
版权所有，侵权必究
举报电话：010-62752024　电子信箱：fd@pup.pku.edu.cn
图书如有印装质量问题，请与出版部联系，电话：010-62756370

前　言

《旅游英语视听说》（第二版）教学内容涵盖出境旅游全过程，从订票、离境、飞行途中到旅游目的地的住宿、餐饮、交通、游览、购物、娱乐、应急处理等各个方面，自然有趣地再现了旅游不同场景。通过视频、对话、阅读、听力、讲故事，学生不仅能较快地掌握旅游专门用途英语，而且学习了旅游相关专业知识，力争做到旅游语言能力与旅游专业知识的双融通。

教材分8个单元，共16章，包括出行准备、旅行途中、住宿酒店、旅游交通、餐饮服务、观光度假、购物淘宝、投诉应急等内容，涵盖"吃、住、行、游、购、娱"旅游六要素。教材采用视、听、说立体化教学方法，配有多媒体教学内容，设计了多种趣味性强的互动式练习。

教材为旅游英语视听说立体化教材，采用MES（Modules of Employable Skill，就业技能模块）模块式教学设计，适用于旅游英语、空乘英语、英语口语等课程的教学，也可用作企业员工英语口语、研学旅行培训。教材为老师制作了电子课件，需要电子课件的教师，请注明教学单位及姓名，致函ernestzhu@126.com索取。在此，谨向给予我们帮助的中外旅游行业专家和教育工作者表示衷心的感谢。

朱　华
2020年3月

Contents 目录

Unit One　Air Tickets and Boarding 机票与登机

Chapter 1　Reservation for Air Tickets 机票预订 ················· 2
Part One: Know-how for Tourism and Travel 旅游知识 ················· 3
　Travel Agency 旅行社 ················· 3
Part Two: Attractive to Watch 观看学旅游 ················· 4
　Video: How to Save Money When Booking Air Tickets? 如何省钱订机票? ················· 5
Part Three: Amusing to Listen 听说学旅游 ················· 5
　Compound Dictation: E-Ticket 电子机票 ················· 5
Part Four: Interesting to Speak 交谈学旅游 ················· 6
　Dialogue: Flight Reconfirmation 机票重新确认 ················· 6
Part Five: Useful to Expand—Consolidation 巩固练习 ················· 7
　Reading: How to Make Airline Reservations? 如何预订机票? ················· 7
　Story-retelling: I Know It's a Big Animal 我知道它是个大动物 ················· 8

Chapter 2　Airport Check-in 机场登机 ················· 10
Part One: Know-how for Tourism and Travel 旅游知识 ················· 11
　ABC about Airport Check-in 机场登机常识 ················· 11
Part Two: Attractive to Watch 观看学旅游 ················· 12
　Video: How to Get to the Airport on Time? 如何按时到达机场? ················· 13
Part Three: Amusing to Listen 听说学旅游 ················· 13
　Compound Dictation: Online Check-in 网上办理登机手续 ················· 13
Part Four: Interesting to Speak 交谈学旅游 ················· 14
　Dialogue: Inquiry About Weight Limit 行李重量咨询 ················· 14
Part Five: Useful to Expand—Consolidation 巩固练习 ················· 15
　Reading: Expressions Related to Air Travel 航空旅行相关表述 ················· 15
　Story-retelling: Kissing the Luggage Goodbye 与行李吻别 ················· 16

Unit Two　On Route and Arrival 途中与抵达

Chapter 3　Amusement During the Flight 飞行途中的乐趣 ················· 19
Part One: Know-how for Tourism and Travel 旅游知识 ················· 20
　In-flight Services 机上服务 ················· 20

Part Two: Attractive to Watch 观看学旅游 ·· 21
　　Video: How to Recover from Jet Lag? 怎样克服飞行时差综合征? ················ 22
Part Three: Amusing to Listen 听说学旅游 ··· 22
　　Compound Dictation: Useful Tips Onboard 机上有用小贴士 ···················· 22
Part Four: Interesting to Speak 交谈学旅游 ·· 23
　　Dialogue: In-flight TV Programs and Channels 机上电视节目和频道 ············ 23
Part Five: Useful to Expand—Consolidation 巩固练习 ····························· 24
　　Reading: Are Blind Pilots Flying? 盲人飞行员在飞吗? ··························· 24
　　Story-retelling: The Plane Is Crashing into the Ocean 飞机要掉到海里啦 ······· 25

Chapter 4　Preparations Before Landing 飞抵前的准备 ·················· 27

Part One: Know-how for Tourism and Travel 旅游知识 ····························· 28
　　Preparations Before the Plane Lands 飞机降落前的准备 ························ 28
Part Two: Attractive to Watch 观看学旅游 ··· 29
　　Video: United Airlines Touched Down at San Francisco 联合航空公司航班抵达旧金山 ········ 30
Part Three: Amusing to Listen 听说学旅游 ··· 31
　　Compound Dictation: Landing Announcement 飞机降落机场通知 ·············· 31
Part Four: Interesting to Speak 交谈学旅游 ·· 31
　　Dialogue: Proper Way to Fill Out the Forms 正确的填表方法 ··················· 31
Part Five: Useful to Expand—Consolidation 巩固练习 ····························· 32
　　Reading: Instructions on the Declaration Form 报关表须知 ····················· 32
　　Story-retelling: We're Still on the Ground 我们还在地上 ························ 35

Unit Three　Hotel and Accommodation 酒店与住宿

Chapter 5　Reservation and Check-in 预订与入住 ························ 37

Part One: Know-how for Tourism and Travel 旅游知识 ····························· 38
　　Front Desk/Reception Desk 前台 ·· 38
Part Two: Attractive to Watch 观看学旅游 ··· 39
　　Video: Hotel Front Desk Clerk 酒店前台人员 ··································· 39
Part Three: Amusing to Listen 听说学旅游 ··· 40
　　Compound Dictation: Tips for Hotel Reservation 酒店预订技巧 ················ 40
Part Four: Interesting to Speak 交谈学旅游 ·· 41
　　Dialogue: Changing Reservation 改订房间 ······································ 41
Part Five: Useful to Expand—Consolidation 巩固练习 ····························· 42
　　Reading: Documents for Hotel Check-in 入住酒店证件 ························· 42
　　Story-retelling: Don't Treat Us like We're a Couple of Fools 别把我们当成一对傻瓜 ········· 43

Chapter 6 Hotel Check-out 离店结账 ·········· 45

Part One: Know-how for Tourism and Travel 旅游知识 ·········· 46
   ABC for Hotel Check-out 离店结账常识 ·········· 46
Part Two: Attractive to Watch 观看学旅游 ·········· 47
   Video: A Checklist for Check-out 离店结账清单 ·········· 47
Part Three: Amusing to Listen 听说学旅游 ·········· 48
   Compound Dictation: How to Save Money on Hotel Bills? 怎样节省酒店开支? ·········· 48
Part Four: Interesting to Speak 交谈学旅游 ·········· 49
   Dialogue: A Late Check-out 延时退房 ·········· 49
Part Five: Useful to Expand—Consolidation 巩固练习 ·········· 50
   Reading: Avoid Extra Hidden Fees 避免额外的隐性费用 ·········· 50
   Story-retelling: The Hotel Bill 饭店账单 ·········· 52

Unit Four Transportation for Travel 旅游与交通

Chapter 7 Train and Taxi 火车与出租车 ·········· 55

Part One: Know-how for Tourism and Travel 旅游知识 ·········· 56
   Railway in the United States 美国的铁路交通 ·········· 56
Part Two: Attractive to Watch 观看学旅游 ·········· 57
   Video: Cabs in New York City 纽约出租车 ·········· 58
Part Three: Amusing to Listen 听说学旅游 ·········· 59
   Compound Dictation: Travel by Train in the USA 美国火车旅游 ·········· 59
Part Four: Interesting to Speak 交谈学旅游 ·········· 59
   Dialogue: Travel by Taxi 搭乘出租车 ·········· 59
Part Five: Useful to Expand—Consolidation 巩固练习 ·········· 60
   Reading: Interesting Things About Transport 交通工具趣闻 ·········· 60
   Story-retelling: The Train Has Broken Down 火车开不动了 ·········· 62

Chapter 8 Travel by Cruise 邮轮旅行 ·········· 63

Part One: Know-how for Tourism and Travel 旅游知识 ·········· 64
   Cruise Vacation 邮轮度假 ·········· 64
Part Two: Attractive to Watch 观看学旅游 ·········· 65
   Video: How to Cut Down the Costs for Cruise Travel? 如何减少邮轮旅行开支? ·········· 65
Part Three: Amusing to Listen 听说学旅游 ·········· 66
   Compound Dictation: The Cabins of a Liner 邮轮舱位 ·········· 66
Part Four: Interesting to Speak 交谈学旅游 ·········· 67
   Dialogue: Ready for Getting Aboard the Ship 准备登船 ·········· 67
Part Five: Useful to Expand—Consolidation 巩固练习 ·········· 68
   Reading: Water Excursions at Cancun 坎昆水上旅游 ·········· 68

Story-retelling: God Could Not Save Me 上帝救不了我 70

Unit Five　Catering Service 餐饮与服务

Chapter 9　Taking Orders 点菜 72

Part One: Know-how for Tourism and Travel 旅游知识 73
　　American Food 美国菜 73
Part Two: Attractive to Watch 观看学旅游 74
　　Video: Etiquette for Ordering Wine 点葡萄酒的礼仪 75
Part Three: Amusing to Listen 听说学旅游 75
　　Compound Dictation: Table Etiquette 餐桌礼仪 75
Part Four: Interesting to Speak 交谈学旅游 76
　　Dialogue: Taking an Order for Western Food 点西餐 76
Part Five: Useful to Expand—Consolidation 巩固练习 77
　　Reading: Idioms Related to Foods and Drinks 餐饮酒水相关成语 77
　　Story-retelling: Pardon Me, Ma'am 对不起，夫人 78

Chapter 10　Paying the Bill 结账 80

Part One: Know-how for Tourism and Travel 旅游知识 81
　　Tips for Paying the Bill 结账小窍门 81
Part Two: Attractive to Watch 观看学旅游 82
　　Video: How to Tip in a Restaurant? 怎样在饭店付小费？ 83
Part Three: Amusing to Listen 听说学旅游 84
　　Compound Dictation: ABC about Tipping in the USA 美国小费常识 84
Part Four: Interesting to Speak 交谈学旅游 85
　　Dialogue: A Miscalculated Bill 账单出错 85
Part Five: Useful to Expand—Consolidation 巩固练习 86
　　Reading: The Bill's on Who 谁来付钱 86
　　Story-retelling: The Bill 账单 88

Unit Six　Sightseeing and Vacation 观光与度假

Chapter 11　Sightseeing 观光旅游 90

Part One: Know-how for Tourism and Travel 旅游知识 90
　　The Bus Tour 巴士观光旅游 90
Part Two: Attractive to Watch 观看学旅游 91
　　Video: California Surfing 加州冲浪 92
Part Three: Amusing to Listen 听说学旅游 93
　　Compound Dictation: An Unforgettable Trip to Niagara Falls 尼亚加拉瀑布难忘之旅 93

Part Four: Interesting to Speak 交谈学旅游 ·········· 94
    Dialogue: A Guided Tour—Lake Tahoe 景点导游——太浩湖 ·········· 94
Part Five: Useful to Expand—Consolidation 巩固练习 ·········· 95
    Reading: A Tour Itinerary 旅游行程 ·········· 95
    Story-retelling: How Did You Get Away? 你是如何逃脱的? ·········· 97

Chapter 12　Vacation 度假 ·········· 98

Part One: Know-how for Tourism and Travel 旅游知识 ·········· 99
    A Money-and-Time Effective Way to Visit Amusement Parks 省钱省时玩转游乐园 ·········· 99
Part Two: Attractive to Watch 观看学旅游 ·········· 100
    Video: A Travel to Universal Studio of Hollywood 好莱坞环球电影制片公司之旅 ·········· 100
Part Three: Amusing to Listen 听说学旅游 ·········· 101
    Compound Dictation: Yosemite National Park 优山美地国家公园 ·········· 101
Part Four: Interesting to Speak 交谈学旅游 ·········· 101
    Dialogue: Walking in the Wall Street 漫步华尔街 ·········· 101
Part Five: Useful to Expand—Consolidation 巩固练习 ·········· 102
    Reading: A Brief History of Disneyland 迪士尼游乐园简介 ·········· 102
    Story-retelling: Roller Coaster 过山车 ·········· 104

Unit Seven　Tourism and Shopping 旅游与购物

Chapter 13　Shopping for Souvenirs 购买纪念品 ·········· 106

Part One: Know-how for Tourism and Travel 旅游知识 ·········· 107
    What to Buy as Souvenir? 买什么做旅游纪念品? ·········· 107
Part Two: Attractive to Watch 观看学旅游 ·········· 108
    Video: What Souvenirs Will Matt Bring Back? 马特会带回什么纪念品? ·········· 108
Part Three: Amusing to Listen 听说学旅游 ·········· 109
    Compound Dictation: Tips for Picking up Souvenirs 选购纪念品的小窍门 ·········· 109
Part Four: Interesting to Speak 交谈学旅游 ·········· 110
    Dialogue: Gifts for My Friends 朋友的礼物 ·········· 110
Part Five: Useful to Expand—Consolidation 巩固练习 ·········· 111
    Reading: Souvenirs in the USA 美国礼品 ·········· 111
    Story-retelling: A Department Store 百货商店 ·········· 113

Chapter 14　Shopping for Clothes 购买衣物 ·········· 114

Part One: Know-how for Tourism and Travel 旅游知识 ·········· 115
    Outlet Shopping 工厂直销店购物 ·········· 115
Part Two: Attractive to Watch 观看学旅游 ·········· 116
    Video: Picking up Discount Clothing 挑选折扣价衣物 ·········· 117

Part Three: Amusing to Listen 听说学旅游 ··· 117
    Compound Dictation: Old-fashioned Outlet Stores 老式工厂直销店 ············· 117
Part Four: Interesting to Speak 交谈学旅游 ··· 118
    Dialogue: A Pair of Pants and a Pair of Shoes 一条裤子、一双鞋 ················ 118
Part Five: Useful to Expand—Consolidation 巩固练习 ····································· 119
    Reading: How Could I Shop at an Outlet? 如何在工厂直销店里购物？ ············ 119
    Story-retelling: Don't Have Any 什么也没有 ··· 120

Unit Eight　Complaints and Emergencies 投诉与应急

Chapter 15　Complaints 投诉 ·· 123
Part One: Know-how for Tourism and Travel 旅游知识 ··································· 123
    Make a Wise and Polite Complaint 有礼有节地投诉 ·································· 123
Part Two: Attractive to Watch 观看学旅游 ··· 124
    Video: A Complaint in the Restaurant 餐厅投诉 ······································· 126
Part Three: Amusing to Listen 听说学旅游 ··· 126
    Compound Dictation: Who Should I Complain to? 我应当向谁投诉？ ············ 126
Part Four: Interesting to Speak 交谈学旅游 ··· 127
    Dialogue: Gifts for My Friends 送朋友的礼物 ··· 127
Part Five: Useful to Expand—Consolidation 巩固练习 ····································· 128
    Reading: Customer Service 客户服务 ·· 128
    Story-retelling: I Don't Care 我无所谓 ··· 129

Chapter 16　Emergencies 突发事件 ·· 130
Part One: Know-how for Tourism and Travel 旅游知识 ··································· 131
    Travel Safety 旅游安全 ·· 131
Part Two: Attractive to Watch 观看学旅游 ··· 132
    Video: Tips for Travelers' Security 旅游安全小知识 ··································· 132
Part Three: Amusing to Listen 听说学旅游 ··· 133
    Compound Dictation: Medicines for Travel 旅游必备药品 ··························· 133
Part Four: Interesting to Speak 交谈学旅游 ··· 134
    Dialogue: A Car Accident 车祸事故 ·· 134
Part Five: Useful to Expand—Consolidation 巩固练习 ····································· 134
    Reading: Emergencies 应急知识 ·· 134
    Story-retelling: Let's Make Sure He's Dead 确认他已死亡 ·························· 136

Unit One

Air Tickets and Boarding
机票与登机

- Chapter 1 Reservation for Air Tickets 机票预订
- Chapter 2 Airport Check-in 机场登机

Chapter 1
Reservation for Air Tickets
机票预订

This chapter introduces the topic on reserving air tickets. To begin with, you'll learn some useful words and phrases related to this topic. Then in Part One, you'll learn some important tourism knowledge related to this chapter. In Part Two, through watching the video, you'll learn tips for saving money when you book your air tickets (refer to Video: How to Save Mongy When Booking Air Tickets?). In Part Three, you'll do a compound dictation: E-ticket. Moreover, in Part Four, through listening to the dialogue, you'll learn how to reconfirm an international air ticket with an airline (refer to Dialogue). Finally, in Part Five, you'll get a chance to expand your knowledge with interesting types of exercises, including readings and story-retelling (refer to Consolidation).

Useful Words and Expressions

retail: （零售）the sale of goods to ultimate consumers, usually in small quantities

devote to: （致力于，专心）to give up (oneself, one's time, energy, etc.) to

specialize in: （专攻，专门研究）to give special or particular attention to

commercial: （商业的）of or for commerce

headquarter: （总部，司令部）place from which (e.g. police or army) operations are controlled

discount: （折扣）amount of money which may be taken off the full price, e.g. of goods bought by shopkeepers for resale of an account if paid promptly, of a bill of exchange not yet due for payment

commission: （佣金）payment for sb. for selling goods etc. rising in proportion to the results gained

reservation: （预定）travel arrangement to keep sth. for sb. e.g. a seat in a train or aircraft, a passage on a ship, a room in a hotel

electronic: （电子的）of electrons, operated by, based on electrons

virtually: （事实上）being in fact, acting as, what is described, but not accepted openly

assign: （分派）to give for use or enjoyment or as a share or part in distribution e.g. of work, duty

departure: （出发）an act of leaving

boarding pass: （登机牌）a pass that authorizes a passenger to board an aircraft and is issued after one's ticket has been purchased or collected

eliminate: （除去，剔除）to remove, take or put away, get rid of

Part One: Know-how for Tourism and Travel
旅游知识

Travel Agency 旅行社

A travel agency is a retail business, selling travel-related products and services to customers. It represents suppliers, such as airlines, car rentals, cruise lines, hotels, railways, sightseeing tours and package holidays. In addition to dealing with ordinary tourists, most travel agencies have a separate department devoted to making travel arrangements for business travelers. Some specialize in commercial and business travel only. Some serve as general sales agents for foreign travel companies, allowing them to have branch offices in different countries from their headquarters.

The British company, Cox & Kings, is said to be the oldest travel agency in the world. Modern travel agencies begin with Thomas Cook in the late 19th century. Brownell Travel in 1887 is the oldest one in North America. With the development of commercial aviation from the 1920s, travel agencies become more popular.

As the name implies, a travel agency's main function is to act as an agent. Its profit is the difference between the advertised price paid by customers and the discounted price provided by suppliers. This is known as the commission. A British travel agent would consider a 10-12% commission as a good arrangement. In the United States, most airlines pay no commission at all to travel agencies. Travel agencies, in this case, usually add a service fee to the net price.

Reservation through travel agencies is a traditional way. Since the process of planning your trips and looking forward to new adventures is an exciting experience, finding a travel agent that meets your needs will help to make your dreams come true.

Read the passage aloud, decide whether the following statements are true or false. Write T for true and F for false.

1. _____ A travel agency is a retail business, dealing with ordinary tourists, and not with business travelers.
2. _____ Some travel agencies serve as general sales agents for foreign travel companies, allowing the existence of branch office in different countries.
3. _____ The American company, Cox & Kings, is said to be the oldest travel agency in the world.
4. _____ The commission of travel agencies is the difference between the advertised price paid by customers and the discounted price provided by suppliers.
5. _____ In the United States, most airlines pay no commission at all to travel agencies.

Part Two: Attractive to Watch
观看学旅游

Brief information from the video

Consider Flying in Off-Peak Times: Flexibility is the key to an inexpensive getaway. Discounts can be found during off-peak times and seasons.

考虑非高峰时期乘坐飞机：灵活变通是廉价出行的关键。非高峰时段和淡季出行可以打折。

Try Flying into Nearby Airports: Once you pick a city, consider flying into nearby airports. Sometimes you can save a bundle arriving into one airport and leaving from another.

尝试前往临近机场：一旦选定城市，可考虑前往临近机场。有时可以在一个机场到达，回程时从另一个机场离开，这样会省一大笔钱。

Be Flexible with Travel Dates: Research is essential to save your money. There are gobs of great online tools to help you find the lowest fare. Some even send you alerts when prices drop between your favorite cities.

灵活安排旅行时间：旅行攻略是省钱的关键。许多不错的在线工具可以帮你找到最低票价。当你心仪的城市之间机票降价时，一些在线工具甚至会及时发邮件提醒你。

Buy Direct from the Airline: Although these travel sites are great, they charge a service fee of at least $5 when it's time to book. Don't even think about calling an airline to buy a ticket unless you absolutely have to. They all charge fees to talk with someone, in hopes you'll complete your purchase on the Internet.

直接从航空公司购票：尽管在旅游网站预订不错，但预定会收取至少5美元的服务费。除非万不得已，千万别打电话向航空公司购票。他们会收取通话费，还是希望你在网上购票。

Know When to Book Your Flight: The best time to book your tickets may be mid-week. Airlines usually announce fare sales around Wednesday or Thursday, and hike fares on the weekend. If you need to book at the last second, forget this—and snag the best price you can find ASAP.

知道什么时候订票：最佳的订票时间是周中（周二至周四）时间。航空公司通常大约在周三或周四公布票价，而周末票价最贵。如果你需要在最后一刻订票，就忘了这一点吧——尽快抢最低的票价吧。

Sign Up for E-mail Alerts: Speaking of last minute tickets, you can find impressive bargains when booking just before take-off. The airlines offer e-mail blasts once a week. And every penny you save getting there is one you can spend once you arrive. Thanks for watching.

注册电子邮件提醒：提到最后一刻订票，你可以在飞机起飞前买到非常便宜的特价票。航空公司每周会群发一次电子邮件。省下的每一分钱，你都可以在抵达目的地后开心享用。谢谢收看。

Video:

How to Save Money When Booking Air Tickets? 如何省钱订机票？

1 Watch the short video twice, and repeat the underlined sentences by heart.

1) _____
2) _____
3) _____
4) _____
5) _____

2 Watch the video again, and review the main contents using the headings of the text.

Part Three: Amusing to Listen
听说学旅游

Compound Dictation:

1 Listen to the passage twice and fill in the blanks with the information you hear (one word for one blank).

E-Ticket 电子机票

An e-ticket is a _____ electronic document used for ticketing passengers, particularly in the commercial airline industry. Virtually, all major airlines now use this method of ticketing.

When a customer books a _____ by telephone or using the Web, the details of the reservation are stored in a computer. The customer can request that a _____ confirmation be sent by postal mail, but it is not needed at the check-in desk. A confirmation number is _____ to the passenger, along with the flight number, date, _____ location, and destination location. When checking in at the airport, the passenger simply presents positive _____. Then necessary boarding passes are issued, and the passenger can check luggage and proceed through _____ to the gate area.

The _____ advantage of e-ticketing is the fact that it reduces booking _____ by eliminating the need for printing and mailing paper documents. Another advantage is that it eliminates the possibility of _____ documents getting lost in the mail or being sent to the wrong address.

2 Talk about the e-tickets with the words that you've filled.
1) _____
2) _____
3) _____

Part Four: Interesting to Speak
交谈学旅游

Dialogue: Flight Reconfirmation 机票重新确认

1 Listen to the situational dialogue carefully, and match the information in column A with that in column B.

Column A	Column B
1. reason for calling	A. Orlando, Florida
2. flight number	B. 11:43 p.m.
3. leaving date	C. to reconfirm the flight
4. destination	D. May 11th
5. local time when arriving	E. 1079

2 Listen to the dialogue again, and role play it in pairs.

Clerk: United Airline, can I help you?

Peter: Hello, I'd like to reconfirm my flight, please.

Clerk: May I have your name and flight number, please?

Peter: My name is Peter, Peter Wilson, and my flight number is 1079.

Clerk: When are you leaving?

Peter: On May 11th.

Clerk: And your destination?

Peter: Orlando, Florida.

Clerk: Hold the line, please. (…) All right. Your seat is confirmed, Mr. Wilson. You will be arriving in Orlando, Florida at 11:43 p.m. local time.

Peter: Thank you. Can I pick up the ticket when I check in?

Clerk: Yes, but please check in at least one hour before departure time.

Peter: O.K. Thank you, and have a nice day!

Part Five: Useful to Expand—Consolidation
巩固练习

Reading:

How to Make Airline Reservations? 如何预订机票？

1. Read the passage below and decide whether the following statements are true or false. Write T for true and F for false.

With the explosion of the Internet, calling the airline reservation desk to book a flight is no longer necessary—in fact, it may cost more. Many airlines are now charging fees to book through a phone representative, encouraging customers to go online, either directly to the airline's website, or to the many airline ticket comparison and booking sites on the web. No matter how you decide to reserve your ticket, browsing the Internet for tickets before you book can save you money.

Identify the specific flight you want. No matter which method you choose to reserve or book your tickets, the process will go faster and be cheaper if you know the exact flight information. By using the Internet to find your ticket, you can save a considerable amount of money. Start on a site such as SideStep.com, FareCompare.com or Priceline.com. With these sites you can compare all airlines that fly to your destination simply by entering your desired departure and arrival information.

Once you've found a ticket at the time and price you want, don't reserve it just yet. Visit Farecast.live.com, a site that not only compares ticket prices, but also makes predictions about whether ticket prices will fall or rise before your departure. Enter your departure and arrival information to get Farecast's advice on whether to purchase/reserve your ticket now or wait.

Visit the airline's website directly. Here you will find specific information about reserving the ticket you want. If you choose to reserve your ticket over the phone, you can visit the airline's website to find out if there is an extra charge to do so.

Check the terms and conditions of your ticket reservation. This is also something that can be done on the website of the airline from which you decide to purchase your ticket. This information will tell you if you can change or cancel your ticket, and if penalties or charges will apply in this situation.

When ready to book your flight, use the airline's website or reservation desk (by phone) to do so, rather than using a third-party site or agent. Booking on the airline's website will typically save you money over using price comparison sites or travel agents, as both typically charge additional booking fees.

1) _____ Many airlines now encourage customers to go online directly to their own websites to book the ticket.
2) _____ You can reserve the ticket once you find a ticket at the time and price you want.
3) _____ Sites such as SideStep.com or Priceline.com can help you compare ticket prices to your destination by entering your departure and arrival information.
4) _____ FareCompare.com can not only let you compare ticket prices but also predict the rising or falling of ticket prices before your departure.
5) _____ You'd better make sure whether there would be an extra charge for booking the ticket over the phone.
6) _____ Booking on the airline's website and through the travel agents typically charge additional booking fees.

Word Tips
explosion	剧增	reservation	预订
browse	浏览	prediction	预测
penalty	惩罚		

2. Discuss: What are the advantages of booking air tickets online?

With the wonders of technology and the creation of the world-wide-web, the world seems to be a smaller place than before and life has become simpler; booking air tickets has never been so easy before. If you are one of those who still think that booking air tickets is a tough task, you have to take some time in finding out how easy and how great it is to get good flight deals online.

Lead-in Questions:
1) Do you think booking air tickets online is a convenient way?
2) In what way do you think it is convenient?
3) How do you understand that security is another advantage when booking air tickets online?
4) In what way can booking online help you to save money?
5) How do you understand that booking online is a time-saving way?

Group Work: What are the advantages of booking air tickets online?
Step 1: Divide the class into groups.
Step 2: Ask students to discuss the above questions in detail.
Step 3: Have some groups to give their presentations in front of the class.

Story-retelling:

Listen to the funny story and retell it using your own words. You may refer to the key words or phrases given in the box.

Hippopotamus	was at a loss	flight	searching	looked up
airport code	retorted	scoured	offered	Buffalo

I Know It's a Big Animal 我知道它是个大动物

A woman called to make reservations, "I want to go from Chicago to Hippopotamus, New York." The agent was at a loss for words. Finally, the agent asked, "Are you sure that's the name of the town?"

"Yes, what flights do you have?" replied the customer. After some searching, the agent came back and said, "I'm sorry, ma'am, I've looked up every airport code in the country and can't find a Hippopotamus anywhere."

The customer retorted, "Oh don't be silly. Everyone knows where it is. Check your map!" The agent scoured a map of the state of New York and finally offered, "You don't mean Buffalo, do you?"

"That's it! I knew it was a big animal!"

Chapter 2
Airport Check-in
机场登机

This chapter introduces the topic on checking in at the airport. To begin with, you'll learn some useful words and phrases related to this topic. Then in Part One, you'll learn some important tourism knowledge related to this chapter. In Part Two, through watching the video, you'll learn wise ways to arrive at the airport on time (refer to Video: How to Get to the Airport on Time?). In Part Three, you'll do a compound dictation: Online Check-in. Moreover, in Part Four, through listening to the dialogue, you'll learn how to ask for weight limit of passenger's luggage (refer to Dialogue). Finally, in Part Five, you'll get a chance to expand your knowledge with interesting types of exercises, including readings and story-retelling (refer to Consolidation).

Useful Words and Expressions

handle: （处理）to manage, deal with, or be responsible for
on behalf of: （代表）as a representative of or a proxy for
domestic: （国内的）of or pertaining to one's own or a particular country as a part from other countries
prior to: （在……之前）before
inquire: （询问）to seek information by questioning; ask
upgrade: （给……升级）to promote to a higher grade or rank
overweight: （超重的）weighing more than is considered normal, proper, etc.
proceed: （继续进行）to go on to do something
inspect: （检查）to look carefully at or over; view closely and critically
stamp: （把……印盖在）to impress with a particular mark or device, as to indicate genuineness, approval, or ownership
lounge: （休息室）a place for sitting, waiting, smoking, etc., esp. a large public room, as in a hotel, theater, or air terminal, often with adjoining washrooms
procedure: （步骤）a particular course or mode of action
abide by: （遵守）to act in accord with
ample: （充足的）fully sufficient or more than adequate for the purpose or needs; plentiful; enough
option: （选择）something that may be or is chosen; choice
prefer: （优先选择）to set or hold before or above other persons or things in estimation
available: （可获得的）readily obtainable; accessible
counterpart: （职位或作用相当的人或物）a person or thing closely resembling another, esp. in function

Part One: Know-how for Tourism and Travel
旅游知识

ABC about Airport Check-in 机场登机常识

Airport check-in is a service found at commercial airports dealing with commercial air travel. The check-in is normally handled by an airline or a handling agent on behalf of an airline.

Check-in at the right counter is the first thing you need to do when arriving at the airport. Although different airlines may have different regulations as to the time of check-in, generally, for an international travel, you'd better arrive and check in at least 2 hours before the scheduled departure time; and for a domestic travel, you should arrive at least thirty minutes prior to the departure. While checking in, you will show your ticket, ID card, or passport and visa. Meanwhile, you can enjoy such services as choosing seats, inquiring about flight or destination information, or paying for upgrades and so on.

If necessary, you can also check in your baggage. The baggage you are allowed to take should be within the weight limit; otherwise, you will have to pay overweight charge, which is usually very high. After getting the boarding pass and paying the airport tax (if it is not included in the ticket), you should proceed to the boarding gate, having your documents inspected and stamped and going through security inspection. Then, you can have a good rest in the lounge until your flight is called.

Occasionally different airlines may have different check-in procedures with some airlines allowing certain restrictions. Sometimes even the same airline at two separate airports may also have different check-in procedures. When one carrier refuses to abide by the procedure that another carrier normally would be willing to do, it will lead to service interruption to passengers. So you'd better leave ample time for check-in.

Read the passage aloud, decide whether the following statements are true or false. Write T for true and F for false.

1. _____ When you arrive at the airport, the first thing you need to do is check-in.
2. _____ If you are taking a domestic travel, you need to arrive at the airport at least 2 hours before the scheduled departure time.
3. _____ You can enjoy such services as choosing seats, inquiring about flight or destination information, or paying for upgrades while checking in.
4. _____ The overweight charge for baggage is within the limlit that you can offer.
5. _____ The same airline at two separate airports always has similar check-in procedures.

Part Two: Attractive to Watch
观看学旅游

Brief information from the video

Catching a flight is tricky. Leave too early and you'll sit at the gate for hours; <u>leave too late and you might miss your plane.</u>

赶飞机是件棘手的事。 去得太早，会在大门口等上几个小时；去得太晚，又可能赶不上飞机。

Confirm your departure time. Confirm your departure time the morning of or the night before your flight, <u>either by calling your airline or by checking online</u>.

确认出发时间。 在乘机前当天早上或晚上，打电话给航空公司或上网查询，确认航班起飞时间。

Visit the Transportation website. Visit the Transportation Security Administration's website at www.tsa.gov for security waiting times at all the major airports. <u>Sign up for updates from your airline's website</u>.

访问运输网站。 访问美国运输安全管理局网站www.tsa.gov，查看主要机场的安检候机时间。及时登录航空公司网站，获取最新资讯。

Listen to the traffic radio. Listen to the traffic report for accidents and construction projects that might slow you down and <u>budget your time accordingly</u>.

收听交通广播。 途中收听可能耽误你出行的交通事故和施工报道，根据情况安排你的时间。

Find out the parking lot. If you're leaving your car at the airport, visit the airport's website to find out exactly where long- and short-term parking is located. Also, map the best route online. <u>Research the best way to get from the parking lot to the main terminal.</u>

寻找停车场。 如果要在机场泊车，事先访问机场网站，寻找长停或短停停车场的准确位置。还要上网查询最佳行车线路，研究停车场到主航站楼的最佳道路。

Pick up or take the bus. If you're getting a ride with a service or even a friend, <u>confirm when and where the driver is picking you up</u>. If you're taking the bus, double-check the schedule.

搭便车或乘公交车。 如果搭乘付费车或坐朋友的车，确认司机来接你的时间和地点。如果坐公交车，仔细检查乘车时刻表。

Confirm the check-in terminal. If you're headed to a big airport, call on your way to <u>confirm that your departure gate and check-in terminal hasn't changed</u>.

确认登机台。 如果去大型机场，你得在途中打电话，确认登机门和登机口是否有变化。

Get the travel documents ready. When you arrive, <u>have your ticket and ID out</u>. It will help get you through check-in faster.

准备好旅行证件。 到达机场时，拿出机票和身份证，这样办理登机手续会快些。

Video:

How to Get to the Airport on Time? 如何按时到达机场？

① Watch the short video twice, and repeat the underlined sentences by heart.

1) _____
2) _____
3) _____
4) _____
5) _____
6) _____
7) _____
8) _____

② Watch the video again, and review the main contents using the headings of the text.

Part Three: Amusing to Listen
听说学旅游

Compound Dictation:

① Listen to the passage twice and fill in the blanks with the information you hear (one word for one blank).

Online Check-in 网上办理登机手续

Online check-in is the process where passengers _____ their presence on a flight via the internet, and typically print their own _____ passes. Depending on the carrier and the _____ flight, passengers may also enter details such as meal options and baggage quantities and select their _____ seating.

This service is generally _____ by the airlines to passengers as being easier and faster because it avoids the need to queue at the airport _____ counter; furthermore, online check-in for a flight is often _____ earlier than its in-person counterpart. Typically, web based check-in for airline travel is offered on the airline's website not earlier than 24 hours before a flight's _____ departure or 7 days for Internet Check-In Assistant. However, some airlines allow a longer time, such as Ryanair which opens online check-in five days beforehand. Depending on the airline, there can be _____ of better seating or upgrades to first/business class offered to the first people to check-in for a flight. In order to meet this demand some sites have offered travelers the ability to _____ an airline check-in prior to the 24-hour window and receive airline boarding passes by email.

2 Talk about the on-line check-in with the words that you've filled.
1) _____
2) _____
3) _____

Part Four: Interesting to Speak
交谈学旅游

Dialogue: Inquiry About Weight Limit 行李重量咨询

1 Listen to the situational dialogue carefully, and match the information in column A with that in column B.

Column A	Column B
1. flight number	A. only one
2. destination	B. economy
3. class	C. 40 lb
4. weight limit	D. UA856
5. number of bags	E. Los Angeles

2 Listen to the dialogue again, and role play it in pairs.

Staff: Good morning. Can I help you?
Bob: Good morning. I'd like to check in for UA 856 to Los Angeles.
Staff: Your passport and ticket, please?

Bob: Here you are. Can I have a window seat?
Staff: Certainly. How many bags do you have?
Bob: Only one.
Staff: Would you please put it on the scale?
Bob: All right. What is the weight limit?
Staff: Well, it depends on the class of your ticket. What class are you traveling?
Bob: Economy class.
Staff: 40 lb.
Bob: I hope my baggage isn't overweight.
Staff: No, it isn't. Here are your boarding pass and baggage claim ticket. Have a good trip!
Bob: Thank you!

Part Five: Useful to Expand—Consolidation
巩固练习

Reading:

Expressions Related to Air Travel 航空旅行相关表述

1. Survey: Take this quiz to find out how much you know about expressions related to air travel. Words in the following box are for your reference.

> baggage claim, gate, carry-on, baggage, aisle seat, window seat, seat assignment, visa, check-in, passport, ticket, reservation, flight number, domestic, international, flight, customs, boarding pass, claim check

1) Document which identifies you as a citizen of a certain country and which allows you to travel to other countries is called a _____.

2) A flight within one country is called a _____ flight.

3) A flight between different countries is called a(n) _____ flight.

4) The letters and numbers which identify an airplane making a specific flight are called a _____.

5) The section of an airport, station, etc., where baggage is checked for contraband and for goods subject to duty is called _____.

6) A printed piece of paper which allows you to travel on an airplane is a _____.

7) The first thing to do at the airport is _____, which means to register as a passenger for a flight.

8) A trip on an airplane is called a _____.

9) A small ticket with printed numbers that identify your baggage is called a baggage _____.

10) Ordering a seat to be held for you on the day you want to travel is called making a _____.

11) The selection of a specific seat for a trip on an airplane is called _____.

12) A seat next to the window in an airplane is called a _____.

13) A seat next to the passage between the rows of seats in an airplane is called an _____.

14) The suitcases and bags which contain your belongings are called _____.

15) The area where you pick up your baggage after a flight is called _____.

16) Stamp in your passport which allows you to travel to another country is called a _____.

17) A printed card which allows you to get on an airplane is called a _____.

18) A door which leads from the airport building into an airplane is called a _____.

19) A bag which you carry with you on the airplane is called a _____ bag.

Word Tips

identify	认出	specific	特定的
register	登记	document	证件
contraband	违禁品	passage	通道
contain	容纳	belongings	财物

2. Discuss: What do you need to do before and after arriving at the airport?

Compared with other means of transportation, traveling by air is more convenient and comfortable. And now more and more people choose this way to travel. However, there are also some troubles, such as the long time spent on check-in. Therefore, it is necessary to make some preparations to ensure a smooth travel experience.

Lead-in Questions:

1) What travel documents should you bring?

2) When will you leave for the airport?

3) How do you know you haven't forgotten anything necessary for the trip?

4) What is the first thing you should do at the airport?

5) If you find there is a long queue in front of the check-in counter, what will you do?

Group Work: What do you need to do before and after arriving at the airport?

Step 1: Divide the class into groups.

Step 2: Ask students to discuss the above questions in detail.

Step 3: Have some groups to give their presentations in front of the class.

Story-retelling:

Listen to the funny story and retell it using your own words. You may refer to the key words or phrases given in the box.

Christmas	decorate	blare	annoying
take...seriously	mood	mistletoe	Picasso sort of way
irritation	vent	luggage scale	

Kissing the Luggage Goodbye 与行李吻别

It was a few days before Christmas. The trip went reasonably well, and he was ready to go back home. The airport had been decorated red and green, and loudspeakers blared annoying renditions of cherished Christmas carols.

Being someone who took Christmas very seriously, and being slightly tired, he was not in a particularly good mood. Going to check in his luggage, he saw hanging mistletoe. Not real mistletoe, but very cheap plastic with red paint on some of the rounder parts and green paint on some of the flatter and pointer parts, that could be taken for mistletoe only in a very Picasso sort of way.

With a considerable degree of irritation and nowhere else to vent it, he said to the attendant, "Even if we were married, I would not want to kiss you under such a ghastly mockery of mistletoe."

"Sir, look more closely at where the mistletoe is."

"Ok, I see that it's above the luggage scale which is the place you'd have to step forward for a kiss."

"That's not why it's there."

"Ok, I give up. Why is it there?"

"It's there so you can kiss your luggage good-bye."

Unit Two

On Route and Arrival
途中与抵达

- Chapter 3 Amusement During the Flight 飞行途中的乐趣
- Chapter 4 Preparations Before Landing 飞抵前的准备

Chapter 3
Amusement During the Flight
飞行途中的乐趣

This chapter introduces the topic on asking for service during the flight. To begin with, you'll learn some useful words and phrases related to this topic. Then in Part One, you'll learn some important tourism knowledge related to this chapter. In Part Two, through watching the video, you'll learn effective ways to recover from jet lag (refer to Video: How to Recover from Jet Lag?). In Part Three, you'll do a compound dictation: Useful Tips Onboard. Moreover, in Part Four, through listening to the dialogue, you'll learn how to ask for information about in-flight entertainment programs and channels (refer to Dialogue). Finally, in Part Five, you'll get a chance to expand your knowledge with interesting types of exercises, including readings and story-retelling (refer to Consolidation).

Useful Words and Expressions

exotic: （异国情调的）of foreign origin or character; not native; introduced from abroad, but not fully naturalized or acclimatized

long-haul: （长途运输的）(esp. of an aircraft flight) covering a long distance around the world

turbulence: （湍流）irregular motion of the atmosphere, as that indicated by gusts and lulls in the wind

category: （类别）any general or comprehensive division; a class

advanced: （高级的）ahead or far or further along in progress, complexity, knowledge, skill, etc.

entertainment: （娱乐）something affording pleasure, diversion, or amusement, esp. a performance of some kind

install: （安装）to place in position or connect for service or use

various: （各种各样的）of different kinds, as two or more things; differing one from another

complimentary: （免费赠送的）given free as a gift or courtesy

headset: （耳机）earphones or headphones

assorted: （各种各样混杂在一起的）consisting of different or various kinds; miscellaneous

formality: （正式手续）accordance with required or traditional rules, procedures, etc.

commodity: （商品）an article of trade or commerce, esp. a product as distinguished from a service

cosmetic: （化妆品）any substance, such as a face cream or body powder, that is intended to make the skin or hair more beautiful

luxury: （奢侈品）something that is very pleasant and enjoyable, but not necessary and not often had or done

contribute to: （有助于）to be an important factor in; help to cause

solve:	（解决）	to find the answer or explanation for; clear up; explain
responsibility:	（责任）	the state or fact of being responsible
be aware of:	（意识到）	having knowledge or understanding
device:	（设备）	a thing made for a particular purpose; an invention or contrivance, esp. a mechanical or electrical one
consult:	（咨询）	to seek advice or information from; ask guidance from
disruptive:	（扰乱性的）	causing, tending to cause, or caused by disruption; disrupting
hydrated:	（含水的）	chemically combined with water in its molecular form
prevent:	（阻止）	to keep from occurring; avert; hinder
stiff:	（僵直的）	(of a person or animal) not supple; moving with difficulty, as from cold, age, exhaustion, or injury
flight attendant:	（空中乘务员）	an airline employee who serves meals, attends to passengers' comfort, etc., during a flight; also called cabin attendant

Part One: Know-how for Tourism and Travel
旅游知识

In-flight Services 机上服务

Vacation is helpful to free us from boring daily routines and various pressures of modern life. However, it also brings us other kinds of pressure. It is exciting and interesting to enjoy exotic scenery and culture, but taking a long-haul international flight is always hard and dull since the flight usually lasts more than 12 hours and passengers have to stay in the small cabin without much move. The journey may become even more miserable if the aircraft comes across some turbulence during the flight. Therefore, in-flight services provided by the airlines are especially important for passengers to kill time and relax themselves. Although the services are somewhat different according to the airlines, cabin classes and the distance of the journey, they can be roughly divided into the following categories.

Entertainment: In the past, entertainment just meant food and drink service. With the development of science and technology, more and more advanced equipment has been installed, which makes it possible for passengers to choose from various offerings, such as movies, TV programs, radio programs and music of different types. You can enjoy whatever you like with a complimentary headset and get relaxed.

Meal and Beverage Service: Such beverages as soft drinks, bottled purified water, milk, tea, assorted fruit juices, etc. are served free of charge while alcoholic beverages are provided free for passengers in first or business class and for purchase for those in economy class. Likewise, passengers in different cabin classes are served different meals. Usually there are several options for you. And those who have special requests can have special meals, but need to place the requests while booking the flight or going through check-in formalities.

Duty Free Shopping: An intercontinental flight offers duty free commodities, such as alcohol, fragrances, cosmetics and some other luxury goods. The price of these goods especially alcohol and tobacco is lower than that in retail shops. You can save much money, but the choice of these products is rather limited.

High-tech services: As mobile phone is not permitted to be used during the flight, you can't keep in touch with your family members and friends. This contributes to your worries. Nowadays, with the offering of satellite phone service and Internet service on international flight, this problem has been totally solved.

Read the passage aloud, decide whether the following statements are true or false. Write T for true and F for false.

1. _____ In-flight services are somewhat different according to the airlines, cabin classes and the distance of the journey.
2. _____ Entertainment means movies, TV programs and radio programs except for food and drink service.
3. _____ Alcoholic beverages are provided free of charge for all passengers during the flight.
4. _____ The price of duty free commodities offered by international flight is higher than that in retail shops.
5. _____ Now satellite phone service and Internet service have been offered on international flight.

Part Two: Attractive to Watch
观看学旅游

Brief information from the video

There are a few things that you could do that I want to share with you today that will help you out in your quest to avoid the doldrums of jet lag.

今天，我想和大家分享一些摆脱时差困扰的事情。

Drink a lot of water. It can be avoided almost entirely by drinking a lot of water. <u>So stay hydrated during your flight</u>. If so, you're going to be having a much better chance of retaining nutrients in your body as well as vitamins and minerals.

多喝水。多喝水，这会帮你倒时差。飞行途中身体保持充足的水分，这样可很好地维持体内的营养、维生素和矿物质。

Set your watch. <u>Set your watch the moment you get on the plane for your new destination.</u>

调时间。上飞机后将手表时间设为目的地时间。

Avoid alcoholic beverages and caffeine. Avoid salty snacks like nuts. <u>Try to sleep as much</u>

as possible on the plane.

不要喝含酒精的饮料和咖啡。不要吃像坚果一类的咸味食品。飞行途中尽量多睡一会儿。

Eat vitamins and stay healthy. Eat vitamins and stay healthy, and you'll overcome that jet lag within a few days.

口服维生素，保持身体健康。 口服维生素，保持身体健康，几天后你就会倒过时差。

Video:

How to Recover from Jet Lag? 怎样克服飞行时差综合征？

1 Watch the short video twice, and repeat the underlined sentences by heart.

1) _____

2) _____

3) _____

4) _____

2 Watch the video again, and review the main contents using the headings of the text.

Part Three: Amusing to Listen
听说学旅游

Compound Dictation:

1 Listen to the passage twice and fill in the blanks with the information you hear (one word for one blank).

Useful Tips Onboard 机上有用小贴士

Pay close attention to the brief safety _____ at the beginning of the flight and know the _____ of all exits. _____ is everyone's responsibility.

Be aware of which electronic devices are and are not allowed to be used during the flight. If you are _____ of the rules, consult a crew member.

Follow the instructions of the crew at all times and be _____ of them and the other passengers.

It is _____ to behave in a manner threatening to other passengers on _____ the flight. Remember, everyone has the _____ to travel in a safe and secure environment. _____ the crew of any disruptive behavior, follow their instructions and be polite.

Drinking juice or water during your flight—instead of coffee or alcohol—will help keep you hydrated.

Try doing seated leg _____ throughout the flight to help prevent stiffness.

2 Talk about the useful tips onboard with the words that you've filled.
1) _____
2) _____
3) _____

Part Four: Interesting to Speak
交谈学旅游

Dialogue: In-flight TV Programs and Channels 机上电视节目和频道

1 Listen to the situational dialogue carefully, and match the information in column A with that in column B.

Column A	Column B
1. reason for calling	A. Channel 9
2. discovery channel	B. a glass of grape juice with ice
3. music channel	C. Channel 6 to 8
4. heavy metal	D. want help to find a war movie
5. beverage required	E. Channels 9 to 12

2 Listen to the situational dialogue again, repeat it sentence by sentence, and then role play it in pairs.

John: Flight attendant.
F.A.: Yes, sir. What can I do for you?
John: I'd like to watch a war movie. Could you tell me which channel the movie is on?
F.A.: Ok. Let me see. Channels 1 to 3 offer programs provided by NBC. 4 to 5 are Disney Channels and 6 to 8 are Discovery Channels. I think you'd better browse through these channels to see what programs are on.

John: I see. If I want to listen to some music, which channel should I use?

F.A.: Music is offered from Channel 9 to 12. There are various types of it, like pop, classical, heavy metal, rock and roll.

John: Let me try. Oh, yes. Channel 9 is offering heavy metal. It's so fantastic. Thank you! Would you please give me something cold to drink?

F.A.: Yes. We have purified water, iced tea, juice and coke. Which one do you like?

John: A glass of grape juice with ice, please.

F.A.: Here you are.

John: Sorry to have bothered you.

F.A.: My pleasure.

Part Five: Useful to Expand—Consolidation
巩固练习

Reading:

Are Blind Pilots Flying? 盲人飞行员在飞吗?

1. Read the passage below and decide whether the following statements are true or false. Write T for true and F for false.

One day at a busy airport, the passengers on a commercial airliner are seated waiting for the pilot to show up so they can get under way.

The pilot and copilot finally appear in the rear of the plane and begin walking up to the cockpit through the center aisle. Both appear to be blind. The pilot is using a white cane, bumping into passengers' right and left as he stumbles down the aisle while the copilot is using a guide dog. Both have their eyes covered with sunglasses.

At first, the passengers do not doubt thinking that it must be some sort of practical joke. After a few minutes though, the engines start revolving, and the airplane begins moving down the runway.

The passengers look at each other with some uneasiness. They start whispering among themselves and look desperately to the stewardesses for reassurance.

Yet, the plane starts accelerating rapidly, and people begin panicking. Some passengers are praying, and as the plane gets closer and closer to the end of the runway, the voices are becoming more and more hysterical.

When the plane has less than twenty feet of runway left, there is a sudden change in the pitch of the shouts as everyone screams at once. At the very last moment, the plane lifts off and is airborne.

Up in the cockpit, the copilot breathes a sigh of relief and tells the pilot: "You know, one of these days the passengers aren't going to scream, and we aren't going to know when to take off!"

1) _____ The pilot is blind, so the copilot helps him to the cockpit.
2) _____ Both the pilot and copilot wear sunglasses so that the passengers can't know whether they are really blind or not.
3) _____ At first, the passengers think it is a practical joke and do not take it seriously.
4) _____ When the plane begins moving down the runway, the passengers start to feel uneasy.
5) _____ As the plane gets closer and closer to the end of the runway, the whole cabin falls into complete quietness suddenly.
6) _____ Everyone including the pilots themselves scream at the moment the plane lifts off.
7) _____ The copilot breathes a sigh of relief because at last the plane takes off successfully.
8) _____ According to the copilot, if the passengers do not scream, the pilots won't know when to take off.

Word Tips

pilot	飞行员	cockpit	驾驶舱
bump	碰，撞	stumble	蹒跚而行
revolve	旋转	stewardess	空中小姐
reassurance	安心	accelerate	加速
panic	恐慌	hysterical	歇斯底里的
pitch	声调	airborne	升空的
relief	减轻		

2. Discuss: What kind of image should a trustworthy pilot have?

With the improvement of people's living standard, more and more people choose to travel by air. However, some people are afraid of this because of occasional happenings of air crash. So a trustworthy pilot can always play an important role to make passengers calm and relaxed.

Lead-in questions:
1) Can you imagine how the pilot and copilot in the story dress themselves?
2) If you take the plane in the story, what will you feel when you see these two pilots?
3) What do you think a pilot should wear?
4) What qualities do you think a good and reliable pilot should have?

Group work: What kind of image should a trustworthy pilot have?
Step 1: Divide the class into groups.
Step 2: Ask students to discuss the above questions in detail.
Step 3: Have some groups to give their presentation in front of the class.

Story-retelling:

Listen to the funny story and retell it using your own words. You may refer to the key words or phrases given in the box.

rough	ocean	fasten	crash	engines
sharks	gel	emergency	rub	enjoy

The Plane Is Crashing into the Ocean 飞机要掉到海里啦

The plane has a pretty rough time above the ocean. Suddenly a voice comes over the intercom, "Ladies and gentlemen, please fasten your seat belts and assume crash positions. We have lost our engines and we are trying to put this baby as gentle as possible down on the water."

"Oh stewardess! Are there any sharks in the ocean below?" asks a little old lady, terrified.

"Yes, I'm afraid there are some. But don't worry. We have a special gel in the bottle next to your chair designed especially for emergencies like this. Just rub the gel onto your arms and legs."

"And if I do this, the sharks won't eat me anymore?" asks the little lady.

"Oh, they will eat you all right, only they won't enjoy it so much."

Chapter 4
Preparations Before Landing
飞抵前的准备

This chapter introduces the topic on the preparations before landing. To begin with, you'll learn some useful words and phrases related to this topic. Then in Part One, you'll learn some important tourism knowledge related to this chapter. In Part Two, through watching the video, you'll learn what you should do before landing and arriving at the international airport (refer to Video: United Airlines Touched Down at San Francisco). In Part Three, you'll do a compound dictation: Landing Announcement. Moreover, in Part Four, through listening to the dialogue, you'll learn how to fill in the forms properly (refer to Dialogue). Finally, in Part Five, you'll get a chance to expand your knowledge with interesting types of exercises, including readings and story-retelling (refer to Consolidation).

Useful Words and Expressions

prior to:	（在……之前）	preceding; before
distribute	（分发, 分配）	to divide and give out in shares; deal out; allot
perforate:	（有孔的）	pierced with a hole or holes
portion:	（部分）	a part of any whole, either separated from or integrated with it
coupon	（票据）	one of a set of detachable certificates that may be torn off and redeemed as needed
procedure:	（办事程序; 步骤）	an act or a manner of proceeding in any action or process; vertical, as in position or posture
standstill:	（停顿）	a state of cessation of movement or action
switch off:	（关掉）	the act or process of switching off a power supply, light source, appliance, etc.
designate:	（指定, 标明）	to mark or point out; indicate; show; specify
content:	（内有的物品）	something that is contained
fill out:	（填写）	to write all the necessary information on an official document, form etc
capital letter:	（大写字母）	a letter of the alphabet that usually differs from its corresponding lowercase letter in form and height, as A, B, Q, and R as distinguished from a, b, q, and r: used as the initial letter of a proper name, the first word of a sentence, etc.
tray table:	（小餐桌）	a tray mounted on or in a piece of furniture, such as an airplane seatback, designed to fold or swing out of the way for storage

Part One: Know-how for Tourism and Travel
旅游知识

Preparations Before the Plane Lands 飞机降落前的准备

Prior to landing at any U.S. international airport, flight attendants distribute two forms to passengers (except American citizens and green card holders): a Customs Declaration Form (6059B) used to declare the value of any gifts or business items that passengers have brought with them to the U.S and the Arrival-Departure Record Form (I-94). Form I-94 has two specific perforated sections in it. The top portion is the arrival form that asks for information related to your arrival in the U.S. The bottom portion is a departure coupon and must be returned to the U.S. officers upon exiting the U.S. The back side of the I-94 form is for government use only. Flight attendants also assist you with your proper completion. You will have to fill out some of your personal information like name, date of birth, passport number, your contact address in the U.S., etc. Fill out the forms using capital letters wherever they mention TYPE or PRINT, which means you should write in capital letters. The forms should be completed before landing.

Approaching the destination, the pilot may come on the loud speaker and announce the airplane is approaching the destination and let you know what the local time is, how the weather is at the destination. Flight attendants will speak on the loud speaker, reminding you of safety procedures such as buckling up seat belts, putting seats in an upright position and turning off electronic devices.

Flight attendants will go about the plane, checking to make sure you fasten the seat belt, seat in an upright position, and tray tables are locked up. They also make sure that all laptop computers and other electronic devices are turned off.

Read the passage aloud, decide whether the following statements are true or false. Write T for true and F for false.

1. _____ Prior to landing at any U.S. international airport, flight attendants distribute one form to passengers.
2. _____ Flight attendants distribute forms to passengers except American citizen and green card holders.
3. _____ A departure coupon must be returned to the U.S. officers upon exiting the U.S.
4. _____ The customers have to fill in both sides of the Arrival-Departure Record Form.
5. _____ All laptop computers and other electronic devices should be turned off when approaching the destination.

Part Two: Attractive to Watch
观看学旅游

Brief information from the video

Clear the immigration. The spirit of warm San Francisco springs from the city's cultural and commercial diversity. The airport has a north and south terminal, a central terminal and an international terminal. Most international flights arrive at concourse G of the international terminal. Because this is an international flight, <u>all passengers must clear US immigration, claim their baggage and clear US customs in San Francisco.</u>

办理入境手续。友好温馨的旧金山精神源于这座城市的文化和商业的多样性。机场有北航站楼、中央航站楼和一个国际航站楼。大多数国际航班抵达国际航站楼G停机坪。我们是国际航班,乘客必须在旧金山办理美国入境手续、领取行李和办理通关手续。

Complete the US custom declaration form. Upon entering immigration, you will be directed to the appropriate lane. <u>Every arriving passenger must complete the US custom declaration form in English in full.</u> If the family is travelling together, the head of the household must complete the form. Please have your passport and completed travel documents ready for the immigration officer. All food and agricultural products must be declared on the US customs declaration form.

填写美国海关申报单。进入移民局,你会被带到相应的通道。每位抵达乘客必须用英文填写美国海关申报表。如果是一家人出行,户主须填写表格。准备好护照和填写好的旅行证件,交给移民局官员检查。所有携带的食品和农产品必须在美国海关申报单上填写申报。

Write only in capital letters. All forms must be completed in blue or black ink and write only in capital letters. <u>It is important to accurately complete both the arrival and departure records.</u> If you are completing the green form, you must also complete the back. Be sure to sign the date on the back of the green form.

用大写字母填表。所有表格必须用蓝色或黑色墨水、用大写字母书写。准确填写抵达和离境记录很重要。填写绿表,背面也需填,记着在背面签上日期。

Ask for assistance. If you need help completing the forms, <u>please ask your flight attendant or United Airlines representative for assistance.</u> Detailed instructions for completing these forms can be found in the back of your *Hemisphere* magazine.

寻求帮助。如果需要他人帮助填表,请向空乘人员或美联航公司代表求助。在《半球》杂志的背面你可以找到填表的详细说明。

Reclaim the baggage. After clearing the immigration, proceed to the baggage claim area to reclaim your baggage. All passengers including those connecting to another flight must claim their baggage. <u>After collecting your baggage, proceed to US customs and agriculture</u>, and have your completed U.S. costumes form ready for the inspector.

领取行李。办理出入境手续后,前往行李处提取行李。所有乘客包括其他转机的乘客必须

29

提取行李。提取行李后，到美国海关、农业检疫部门将填好的表格交给官员检查。

Connect the domestic flights. <u>Passengers with connecting domestic flights will recheck their baggage.</u> Look for flight information monitors for your departure gate. United Airline's domestic flights operate from the north terminal, concourse F. It's an easy walk from the international terminal to United tickets counters and gates located in concourse F. A free shuttle bus service is also provided.

中转国内航班。需要乘坐国内航班转机的旅客将重新托运行李。查看航班信息屏寻找登机口。美联航国内航班在北航站楼F停机坪登机。从国际航站楼到美联航售票处和F停机坪登机口很方便，而且还提供免费穿梭巴士服务。

Provide the airport services. If San Francisco is your final destination, you'll exit Customs to the airport arrival's hall. <u>Currency exchange, car rental services, hotel directories and taxi, ground transportation services are available as you leave.</u> United Airlines is a founding member of the Star Alliance, the world's leading airline alliance.

提供机场服务。如果旧金山是你最终目的地，过海关后去机场到达大厅。机场提供货币兑换、汽车租赁服务、酒店指南、出租车和地面交通服务。美联航是世界领先的航空联盟——星空联盟的创始会员。

Video:

United Airlines Touched Down at San Francisco
联合航空公司航班抵达旧金山

① Watch the short video twice, and repeat the underlined sentences by heart.

1) _____
2) _____
3) _____
4) _____
5) _____
6) _____
7) _____

② Watch the video again, and review the main contents using the headings of the text.

Part Three: Amusing to Listen
听说学旅游

Compound Dictation:

① Listen to the passage twice and fill in the blanks with the information you hear (one word for one blank).

Landing Announcement 飞机降落机场通知

Ladies and gentlemen, welcome to Los Angeles. Please wait until the _____ has come to a _____ standstill before unfastening your _____.

We would like to remind you that mobile phones must _____ completely switched off until the seatbelt _____ has been turned off.

Remember that you can only _____ in designated areas once inside the terminal building.

Please take care when opening the _____ lockers as the contents may have moved during the _____ and might fall out and _____ you or your fellow passengers.

Thank you for flying with us and we look _____ to seeing you onboard with us.

② Talk about the landing announcement with the word or words that you've filled.
1) _____
2) _____
3) _____

Part Four: Interesting to Speak
交谈学旅游

Dialogue: Proper Way to Fill Out the Forms 正确的填表方法

① Listen to the situational dialogue carefully, and match the information in column A with that in column B.

Column A	Column B
1. form-filling requirement	A. black or blue
2. color of ink required	B. didn't write with capital letters
3. reason for asking for a new form	C. capital letters
4. set of forms required for a family	D. one set of form per family
5. person to complete the form	E. head of the household

2 Listen to the dialogue again, and role play it in pairs.

Tom: Excuse me.
F.A.: Yes? How can I help you?
Tom: Could I fill out the form in blue ink?
F.A.: Yes, you can.
Tom: Good. I only have a pen with blue ink.
F.A.: Either black or blue ink is fine.
Tom: All right. Thank you.
F.A.: By the way, don't forget that all the information have to be written in capital letters.
Tom: Oh, I didn't know that. I guess I need a new form. I am sorry.
F.A.: Never mind. Here you are.
Tom: By the way. Did you say all the information had to be written in capital letters?
F.A.: Yes. All the letters should be capitalized.
Tom: I am traveling with my family. Does each one of us have to fill out a custom declaration?
F.A.: No. Only one form per family is required. The head of the household should complete the form.
Tom: I see. Thank you very much.

Part Five: Useful to Expand—Consolidation
巩固练习

Reading:

Instructions on the Declaration Form 报关表须知

1. Read the passage below and decide whether the following statements are true or false. Write T for true and F for false.

Each individual arriving into the United States must complete the CBP Declaration Form 6059B. Explanations for information fields are explained at the end of the sample images.

1) Print your last (family) name. Print your first (given) name. Print the first letter of your

middle name.

2) Print your date of birth in the appropriate day/month/year boxes.

3) Print the number of family members traveling with you (do not include yourself).

4) Print your current street address in the United States. If you are staying at a hotel, include the hotel's name and street address. Print the city and the state in the appropriate boxes.

5) Print the name of the country that issued your passport.

6) Print your passport number.

7) Print the name of the country where you currently live.

8) Print the name of the country (ies) that you visited on your trip prior to arriving to the United States.

9) If traveling by airline, print the airline's name and flight number. If traveling by vessel (ship), print the vessel's name.

10) Mark an X in the Yes or No box. Are you traveling on a business (work-related) trip?

11) Mark an X in the Yes or No box. Are you bringing with you:

a) fruits, plants, food, or insects?

b) meats, animals, or animal/wildlife products?

c) disease agents, cell cultures, or snails?

d) soil or have you visited a farm/ranch/pasture outside the United States?

12) Mark an X in the Yes or No box. Have you or any family members traveling with you been in close proximity of (such as touching or handling) livestock outside the United States?

13) Mark an X in the Yes or No box. Are you or any family members traveling with you bringing $10,000 or more in U.S. dollars or foreign equivalent in any form into the United States?

Read definition of monetary instruments on the reverse side of the form.

Examples: *coins, cash, personal or cashier's check, traveler's checks, money orders, stocks, bonds.*

If yes, you must complete the Customs Form 4790.

14) Mark an X in the Yes or No box. Are you or any family members traveling with you bringing commercial merchandise into the United States?

Examples: *all articles intended to be sold or left in the United States, samples used for soliciting orders, or goods that are not considered personal effects.*

15) If you are a U.S. resident, print the total value of all goods (including commercial merchandise) you or any family members traveling with you have purchased or acquired abroad (including gifts for someone else, but not items mailed to the United States) and are bringing into the United States.

Note: *U.S. residents are normally entitled to a duty-free exemption of $800 on items accompanying them.*

If you are a *visitor (non-U.S. Resident)*, print the total value of all goods (including commercial merchandise) you or any family members traveling with you are bringing into the United States and will remain in the United States.

Note: *Visitors (non-U.S. Residents) are normally entitled to an exemption of $100.*

Declare all articles on this form. For gifts, please indicate the retail value. Use the reverse side of this form if additional space is needed to list the items you will declare.

The U.S. Customs officer will determine duty. Duty will be assessed at the current rate on the first $1,000 above the exemption.
- Read the notice on the reverse side of the form.
- Sign the form and print the date.
- Keep the complete form with you and hand it to the CBP inspector when you approach the Customs and Border Protection area.

Controlled substances, obscene articles, and toxic substances are generally prohibited entry.

1) _____ The number of family members traveling together should include the head of the household.
2) _____ If you are staying at a hotel, you don't have to write down the hotel's name and street address.
3) _____ If you travel by airline, you should print the airline's name and flight number.
4) _____ Visitors (non-U.S. Residents) are normally entitled to an exemption of $100.
5) _____ Keep the complete form with you and hand it to the CBP inspector when you leave the USA.
6) _____ If you travel with other immediate family members, you just need to complete one form.

Word Tips

immediate family	直系亲属	appropriate	适当的
issue	发行	vessel	船
ranch	农场	merchandise	商品
entitled	有资格的	exemption	免税
proximity	附近	livestock	牲畜
equivalent	等同物	obscene	猥亵的
toxic	有毒的	substance	物质

2. Discuss: How to deal with the customs declaration form?

Prior to landing at any U.S. international airport, flight attendants distribute the Customs Declaration Form to passengers. Passengers should complete these forms before landing.

Lead-in Questions:
1) Why do passengers have to fill out the customs declaration?
2) When should the form be ready?
3) What should you do if you are not sure what items should be declared?
4) What problems may you have if the form is not filled out properly?
5) When you have difficulties filling out the form, what will you do?

Group Work: How to deal with the customs declaration form?

Step 1: Divide the class into groups.
Step 2: Ask students to discuss the above questions in detail.
Step 3: Have some groups to give their presentations in front of the class.

Story-retelling:

Listen to the funny story and retell it using your own words. You may refer to the key words or phrases given in the box.

read	air accident	ride	worry
persuade	board the plane	start the engine	dangerous
take-off and landing	frighten	ant	on the ground

We're Still on the Ground 我们还在地上

Mr. Johnson had never been up in an airplane before and he had read a lot about air accidents, so one day when a friend offered to take him for a ride in his own small plane, Mr. Johnson was very worried about accepting. Finally, however, his friend persuaded him that it was very safe, and Mr. Johnson boarded the plane.

His friend started the engine and began to taxi onto the runway of the airport. Mr. Johnson had heard that the most dangerous part of a flight were the take-off and the landing, so he was extremely frightened and closed his eyes.

After a minute or two he opened them again, looked out of the window of the plane, and said to his friend, "Look at those people down there. They look as small as ants, don't they?"

"Those are ants," answered his friend. "We're still on the ground."

Unit Three

Hotel and Accommodation
酒店与住宿

- Chapter 5 Reservation and Check-in 预订与入住
- Chapter 6 Hotel Check-out 离店结账

Chapter 5
Reservation and Check-in
预订与入住

This chapter introduces the topic on the hotel reservation and check-in. To begin with, you'll learn some useful words and phrases related to this topic. Then in Part One, you'll learn some important tourism knowledge related to this chapter. In Part Two, through watching the video, you'll get to know major qualifications of front clerks working in hotels and resorts (refer to Video: Hotel Front Desk Clerk). In Part Three, you'll do a compound dictation: Tips for Hotel Reservation. Moreover, in Part Four, through listening to the dialogue, you'll learn how to make changes for a reservation (refer to Dialogue). Finally, in Part Five, you'll get a chance to expand your knowledge with interesting types of exercises, including readings and story-retelling (refer to Consolidation).

Useful Words and Expressions

beverage: （酒水）(formal) any sort of drink except water, e.g. milk, tea, wine, beer

cashier: （出纳员/收银员）person who receives and pays out money in a bank, store, hotel, restaurant, etc.

accumulate: （累积）make or become greater in number or quantity

transaction: （交易）a piece of business that is done between people, especial an act of buying or selling

register: （登记）make a written and formal record of, in a list

crucial: （关系重大的）decisive; critical

entail: （使必要）make necessary; impose (expense, etc. on sb.)

recession: （不景气）slackening of business and industrial activity

check out: （离店结账）to vacate and pay for one's quarters at a hotel

double room: （双人房间）a type of hotel accommodation with two beds, or sometimes a double bed, for occupancy by two person

single room: （单人房间）a type of hotel accommodation with one bed for occupation by one person

limousine: （豪华轿车）any large, luxurious automobile, esp. one driven by a chauffeur

Part One: Know-how for Tourism and Travel
旅游知识

Front Desk/Reception Desk 前台

Front Desk is also called Reception Desk. It is the nerve center of a hotel. Its major function is to act as the public face of a hotel, primarily by greeting hotel guests and checking in guests. It also provides assistance and services to guests during their stay, completes their accommodation, food and beverage, account and receives payment from guests.

Functions of a Front Desk can be grouped into five general categories:
- reception
- bell service
- mail and information
- concierge
- cashiers and night auditors

There will be two major departments involved in the above list. Employees staffing the first four categories belong to room department. Employees working in the fifth category belong to financial department, where guest charges are accumulated and posted to bills, and all cash transactions are accomplished.

Staff of Front Desk welcome you, carry your luggage, help you register, give you the room keys and mail, answer questions about the activities in the hotel and surrounding area, handle complaints, and finally check you out. They have the responsibility to make you a great first impression on the hotel and make you feel you are very welcomed. Their positive impression made on you will be crucial to a hotel's success. It is of importance for them to be able to work quickly and efficiently to follow all steps to get you check into the hotel. Moreover, they should be knowledgeable about check-out time, hotel service, local attraction and more.

Read the passage aloud, decide whether the following statements are true or false. Write T for true and F for false.

1. _____ Front desk is different from reservation desk.
2. _____ The major function of a front desk is to act as a public face of the hotel.
3. _____ Functions of a front desk can be grouped into five categories; and front desk involves three departments.
4. _____ Front desk should make a great first impression on the hotel so that you feel you are welcomed.
5. _____ Front desk should be knowledgeable about check-out time only.

Part Two: Attractive to Watch
观看学旅游

Brief information from the video

Make a great impression. The front desk clerk is usually the first person a guest encounters when checking in a hotel or motel. In addition to performing the specific duties, he has the responsibility of making a great first impression. It is important for him to be able to quickly and efficiently follow the steps to get the guest check in.

留下好印象。前台接待人员往往是客人在酒店或汽车旅馆入住登记遇到的第一个人。因此除提供各项具体服务外，给客人留下美好的第一印象是其职责所在。对于前台人员来讲，按程序快速高效地让客人入住酒店很重要。

To be knowledgeable. It's essential for him to be knowledgeable about the checking-out times, hotel services and local attractions. What's more, he should have qualities such as: personal warmth, friendliness, and good people skills.

万事通。前台人员应熟悉退房时间、酒店服务项目和当地旅游景点。此外，应热情好客、乐于助人、善于沟通。

Extend a warm welcome. He should make the tired and stressed customers feel truly welcomed and comfortable when they reach hotels so that they'll make a point of staying at the hotel.

热情迎客。旅客舟车劳顿、疲惫不堪。倘若前台让其感到宾至如归，客人便会安心入住。

Customer relations. The front desk is an excellent place to start if you are interested in career of hotel management since you can learn about many different aspects involved in running a hotel efficiently and it places you on the front line of customer relations.

客户关系。如果你有意在酒店管理行业发展，从前台做起再好不过了。在这里你会学到经营管理酒店的方方面面，身临一线，接触客人，学会处理客户关系。

Video:

Hotel Front Desk Clerk 酒店前台人员

1 Watch the short video twice, and repeat the underlined sentences by heart.

1) _____

2) _____

3) _____
4) _____

② Watch the video again, and review the main contents using the headings of the text.

Part Three: Amusing to Listen
听说学旅游

Compound Dictation:

① Listen to the passage twice and fill in the blanks with the information you hear (one word for one blank).

Tips for Hotel Reservation 酒店预订技巧

You can almost guarantee a great price on any hotel package or airfare by making your _____ very early, at least a month or so before your trip. In this way, you'll be locked into a low price. Additionally, while there may be some _____, look for off-peak deals at most major hotels. This may _____ a mid-week stay. If you're looking for a weekend getaway, consider booking your hotel on a Thursday with a Monday _____. Because hotels are feeling the pinch during this recession just like the rest of us, call them directly and find out what types of packages they're currently offering. They may be willing to present you with a _____ that precisely fits your time frame and _____.

If you really want to save on hotel _____, choose bed-and-breakfast _____, smaller hotels or inns. Remember, they're _____ for your business as well. For example, a two-bedroom suite at an East Hampton Inn during off-peak seasons can be gotten for less than $100 per night. _____ rates typically run close to $300 a night for the very same room. Quite a difference, wouldn't you say?

② Talk about the tips for hotel reservation with the words that you've filled.
1) _____
2) _____
3) _____

Part Four: Interesting to Speak
交谈学旅游

Dialogue: Changing Reservation 改订房间

1 Listen to the situational dialogue carefully, and match the information in column A with that in column B.

Column A	Column B
1. reason for calling	A. Sam Brown
2. caller's name	B. Nov. 1 to Nov. 3
3. original date of reservation	C. make some reservation changes
4. new date of reservation	D. limousine
5. extra service	E. from Nov. 1 to Nov. 4

2 Listen to the dialogue again, and role play it in pairs.

Clerk: Good morning, room reservation. How can I help you?

Sam: Yes, my name is Sam. I made a reservation, but I'd like to make some changes.

Clerk: Under whose name was the reservation made?

Sam: Sam Brown.

Clerk: What was the date of the reservation?

Sam: From Nov. 1 to Nov. 3. But the check-out date should be on Nov. 4. And I need a double room instead of a single room.

Clerk: A double room from Nov. 1 to Nov. 4. Is that correct?

Sam: Yes.

Clerk: Do you need a limousine service?

Sam: That's just what I want. How much does it charge?

Clerk: $40. We have a counter at the airport where our representatives will lead you to the car.

Sam: It sounds nice. I'll take that.

Clerk: Thank you, sir. We look forward to serving you.

Part Five: Useful to Expand—Consolidation
巩固练习

Reading:

Documents for Hotel Check-in 入住酒店证件

1. Read the passage below and decide whether the following statements are true or false. Write T for true and F for false.

While checking in a hotel, you'll need to prove that you are the person who made the reservation either in person, over the phone, or through a travel agency. You are required to provide your identification document such as a driver's license, state ID card or passport. There are two reasons for front desk clerk to require your identification. The first reason is to protect customers from fraudulent credit card use and theft. Requiring identification upon check-in is a way that hotels can ensure that a hotel room was not booked with a stolen credit card. The second reason is to protect your safety. Requiring an ID for check-in is a way to make sure that only registered, paid guests like you are admitted to hotel rooms, and prevents strangers or criminals from compromising the personal safety of those staying in the hotel.

Moreover, you may also need to present a reservation confirmation which can guarantee you a room under any circumstances. If you book a hotel room online, you will usually be e-mailed a confirmation statement with a special confirmation number that guarantees your reservation. If you book over the phone, through a travel agent or in person, you'll often be given a printout with your confirmation number on it. For example, if the hotel has made a mistake and shows no record of your reservation, but you have a printed confirmation from them, they will have to accommodate you even if they are fully booked up. However, not all hotels provide confirmation letters. Some hotels will simply give you a confirmation number of the phone when you make your reservation.

Other documentations that you should have on hand when checking in hotels include the credit card you used to make your reservation, or your checkbook, as well as any letters or licenses pertaining to special medical or personal needs. These include doctor's letters regarding medical conditions or dietary restrictions, and permits for seeing-eye dogs that allow guests to bring their animal guides into hotels with no pet policies.

1) _____ When you check in a hotel, you are required to provide your identification documents.

2) _____ One of the reasons for asking for ID is to ensure that guests are using their own

credit cards.

3) _____ All hotels provide confirmation letters that guarantee guests' reservations.
4) _____ Guests can get a confirmation statement only through internet.
5) _____ The hotel will accommodate you if you have a confirmation statement from them.
6) _____ What you need for hotel check-in are: identification document, reservation confirmation, credit card or check book, and letter for special medical or personal care.

Word Tips

fraudulent	欺诈的	criminal	罪犯
comprise	构成	guarantee	保证
accommodate	提供住宿	pertain to	关于
dietary	饮食的		

2. Discuss: What documents do you need for hotel check-in?

Generally speaking, hotel check-in process is simple, quick and hassle-free. Hotel front desk clerks are friendly and ready to assist guests with any concerns they might have. Yet a smooth and satisfactory check-in also needs your cooperation. Work with your partner and discuss the following.

Lead-in Questions:

1) Have you or any of your friends got any experience of hotel check-in?
2) What are the reasons for presenting your identification?
3) Do you think your reservation confirmation number is important, and why?
4) What will happen if you have the confirmation, yet the hotel does not have your booking record?
5) If you pay your bill in cash or check, will you provide your credit card information when asked, and why?

Group Work: What documents do you need for hotel check-in?

Step 1: Divide the class into groups.
Step 2: Ask students to discuss in detail the above questions.
Step 3: Have some groups to give their presentation in front of the class.

Story-retelling:

Listen to the funny story and retell it using your own words. You may refer to the key words or phrases given in the box.

backwoods	celebrate	anniversary	plush hotel	settle for
fools	because	complain	elevator	

Don't Treat Us like We're a Couple of Fools 别把我们当成一对傻瓜

A couple had lived together in the backwoods for over fifty years. To celebrate their fiftieth anniversary, the husband took his wife to a large city, and they checked in a plush hotel.

The wife said to the bellman, "We refuse to settle for such a small room. No windows, no bed, and no air conditioning."

"But, madam!" replied the bellman.

"Don't 'But madam' me," she continued. "You can't treat us like we're a couple of fools just because we don't travel much, and we've never been to the big city, and never spent the night at a hotel. I'm going to complain to the manager."

"Madam," the bellman said, "this isn't your room; this is the elevator!"

Chapter 6
Hotel Check-out
离店结账

This chapter introduces the topic on the hotel check-out. To begin with, you'll learn some useful words and phrases related to this topic. Then in Part One, you'll learn some important tourism knowledge related to this chapter. In Part Two, through watching the video, you'll see how to make sure that nothing will be left behind when you check out a hotel (refer to Video: A Checklist for Check-out). In Part Three, you'll do a compound dictation: How to Save Money on Hotel Bills. Moreover, in Part Four, through listening to the dialogue, you'll learn how to ask for a late check-out (refer to Dialogue). Finally, in Part Five, you'll get a chance to expand your knowledge with interesting types of exercises, including readings and story-retelling (refer to Consolidation).

Useful Words and Expressions

attendant: （服务员）a person who attends another, as to perform a service
inform: （通知）to give or impart knowledge of a fact or circumstance to
in advance: （预先）ahead in time; beforehand
evaluation: （评估）an act or instance of evaluating or appraising
brochure: （小册子）a pamphlet or leaflet
bellboy: （侍者）a bellhop
corporate: （团体的）pertaining to a united group, as of persons
voucher: （凭证）a document, receipt, stamp, or the like, that gives evidence of an expenditure
acknowledgement: （承认）recognition of the existence or truth of something
arrange: （安排）to prepare or plan
regulation: （规定）a law, rule, or other order prescribed by authority, esp. to regulate conduct
reception desk: （前台）a counter, as at a hotel, at which guests are registered, also called front desk

Part One: Know-how for Tourism and Travel
旅游知识

ABC for Hotel Check-out 离店结账常识

When you check in a hotel, usually the attendant at the reception desk will inform you of the check-out time so that when you need to check out you can do it before that time and avoid being charged extra fee. Generally the check-out time in most hotels is 12 o'clock. And you need to pay half of the daily room rate if you check out between 12 p.m. and 18 p.m. or pay a full day's room rate if you check out after 18 p.m.. However, if you have to require a late check-out, you should contact the reception desk before 10 a.m. on the day of departure. The hotel will usually try to satisfy you for free or with a charge.

In order to avoid spending too much time going through check-out formalities, especially during the high season when there is a crowd of guests checking in or checking out, you'd better call the reception desk at least thirty minutes earlier to inform them so that they can get your bill prepared in advance.

Before you check out, a room attendant may go up and check up the room thoroughly to make sure that everything is all right. In addition, he/she will also check whether you have consumed or damaged anything. If so, he/she will make an evaluation and require you to pay for these items when you check out. The price of every item in the room is printed in the room service brochure. So when you consume something or damage something, you'd better browse through the brochure and find the price of these items so that you can check whether there is a mistake in the bill or not.

Usually a bellboy will be arranged to help you with your luggage when you leave the room. At the reception desk, you need to return the room card and confirm the bill. If there is no mistake, you can sign it and make the payment.

Read the passage aloud, decide whether the following statements are true or false. Write T for true and F for false.

1. _____ Generally, the check-out time in most hotels is 12 o'clock.
2. _____ You need to pay half of the daily room rate if you check out after 18 p.m.
3. _____ If you have to require a late check-out, you should contact the reception desk before 8 a.m. on the day of departure.
4. _____ When you want to check out, you'd better call the reception desk at least thirty minutes earlier to inform them.
5. _____ When you check out, you'll be charged for the items you have consumed or damaged in the room.

Part Two: Attractive to Watch
观看学旅游

Brief information from the video

But take a look at this hotel check-out checklist, and you won't be smacking yourself in the forehead when you get back. Check it out.

花点时间，看看这份退房攻略，你就不会为摞下东西、去而折返而懊恼。一起看看吧。

Take your time packing. Take your time packing before you check out. Allowing yourself a few extra minutes to calmly get everything back into your suitcase will reduce your chances of carelessly forgetting anything. If you're pressed for time, you can always call the front desk and request a late check out, which will often buy you another hour.

花点时间收拾行李。退房前花点时间收拾行李。给自己预留一点时间，静下心来收拾行李，避免遗忘东西。如果时间太紧，你也可以打电话延迟退房，通常能多争取一小时的时间。

Do a complete sweep of the room. Once everything obvious is in your bags, be sure to check all the nooks and crannies. As you're about to leave the room, do one final pass over the entire area – and be sure to check under the covers, too.

细查一次房间。该装的东西都装好，还需检查一下房间角落。离开房间前全面扫视一下房间，务必检查有没有东西被覆盖遗漏了。

Leave a tip to the chambermaid. Leave cash in the amount of three to five bucks per night at a fancy hotel, and one or two at a less fancy joint, and be sure to leave it in a properly marked envelope.

给保洁人员留小费。入住高档酒店，每晚留3—4美元现金作小费，普通酒店每晚1-2美元小费。小费务必装在信封里，做好标记。

Review your entire bill. When checking out, be sure to review your entire bill. Check that all of the charges are exact, and make sure you have a paper statement or receipt to walk away with. Remember that now is the time to dispute anything funky — the second you walk out the door, it gets a little bit tougher.

核对账单。退房时要核对账单，确保所有账目无差错，走时带上对账单或收据。要知道退房时是解决争议的最佳时间。一旦出了酒店，发现问题回来处理就棘手了。

Video:

A Checklist for Check-out 离店结账清单

① Watch the short video twice, and repeat the underlined sentences by heart.

1) _____

2) _____

3) _____

4) _____

5) _____

6) _____

7) _____

8) _____

2 Watch the video again, and review the main contents using the headings of the text.

Part Three: Amusing to Listen
听说学旅游

Compound Dictation:

1 Listen to the passage twice and fill in the blanks with the information you hear (one word for one blank).

How to Save Money on Hotel Bills? 怎样节省酒店开支?

When traveling, the most expensive things are _____ the flight and hotel bills. The following is some steps to save money on hotel _____.

Step 1: To save money on hotel bills, you should ask for the hotel's corporate rate when making a reservation. Corporate rates are often much _____ than the normal room prices and most hotels have these corporate _____.

Step 2: Many hotels require that you stay at least 8 nights per year to _____ for the corporate rate. To get around this, you can write a letter to the hotel using your company's _____. Most hotels will give the corporate rate to anyone who does this.

Step 3: If you are using a travel agent to help you book the room, make sure you get a confirmation number which _____ your room. A travel agent will give you a voucher but this has no _____ acknowledgement from the hotel.

Step 4: To save money on hotel bills, shop around for the best pricing _____.

Speaking with many hotels about their corporate rates is the best way to book a room at a very _____ rate.

2 Talk about how to save money on hotel bills with the words that you've filled.

1) _____
2) _____
3) _____

Part Four: Interesting to Speak
交谈学旅游

Dialogue: A Late Check-out 延时退房

1 Listen to the situational dialogue carefully, and match the information in column A with that in column B.

Column A	Column B
1. guest's name	A. 1:00 p.m.
2. room number	B. too early to go to the airport
3. reason for requiring a late check-out	C. Jill Smith
4. due time for cleaning up the room	D. use the business center, free of charge
5. solution to the problem	E. Room 812

2 Listen to the dialogue again, and role play it in pairs.

Clerk: Good morning, Ms. Can I help you?

Jill: Good morning. I'm Jill Smith in Room 812. I'm leaving today. But Can I check out a little bit late?

Clerk: Why?

Jill: You see, my plane takes off at 6:30 this afternoon. But I don't want to go to the airport so early.

Clerk: It's really a problem. But your room has been reserved, and we have to clean it up before 1:00 p.m. o'clock.

Jill: Then can I leave at 2 o'clock?

Clerk: Well, you can't since the guests will check in at 2:00 p.m. I can arrange you to another room, but according to hotel's regulations, during the high season, you should pay half of the daily room rate if you leave before 6 p.m.

Jill: I don't think it's reasonable. Can I speak to your manager?

Clerk: Ok. I'll call our manager.
Manager: Ms., what can I do for you?
Jill: I'm asking for a late check-out since my plane won't take off until 6:30 p.m.
Manager: (…) Your room has been reserved for a newly married couple, and they'll check in at 2:00 p.m. How about going to our business center, free of charge?
Jill: Thank you. That helps me a lot.
Manager: My pleasure. Hope to serve you better next time.

Part Five: Useful to Expand—Consolidation
巩固练习

Reading:

Avoid Extra Hidden Fees 避免额外的隐性费用

1. Read the passage below and decide whether the following statements are true or false. Write T for true and F for false.

Checking out sometimes can give you a serious case of shock. With taxes, room service, phone charges and other "hidden" fees, that $199 deal you booked online can turn into a $379 bill. Keep these tips in mind on your next stay to keep your hotel bill within your budget.

Telephone Charges:

Check what the phone charges are at each hotel you stay in. Many hotels charge as much as $1.50 per minute (or more) for local phone calls. And long distance rates can be unconscionably high. Before you make a call, check the rates. They should be posted somewhere in the room. If you don't see them, call the front desk and ask. Better yet, use your cell phone for all calls, even local.

Room Service:

Room service is expensive. An "American Breakfast" (two eggs, bacon, toast, coffee and juice) can cost upwards of $30. Avoid ordering it if possible. Walk down to the hotel restaurant to order, or better yet, walk down the street.

When you do order room service, pay close attention to the fees tacked on to the bill. Many hotels charge a "delivery charge" of several dollars added to the already steep prices. Plus, most room service bills automatically add a 15—18 percent gratuity. Overlooking this can cause you to over-tip, so beware.

Internet Access:

Many hotels are adding high-speed Internet access to their amenities. This is a great service if you are doing a lot of work online while on the road. Be aware that there is usually a charge for this service (generally $10 per day). If you have the time, it's cheaper to stop in at a nearby coffee shop that offers free Wi-Fi. Also, many hotels that charge for Internet access in the rooms offer it free of charge in the lobby, so ask.

Mini Bar:

If you have late-night food cravings, plan ahead and pack accordingly. Otherwise, that 3 a.m. Snickers bar may cost you five bucks. The honor bar tempts you by stocking tasty snacks, alcohol and other luxuries right in your room for convenience, but you are definitely paying for it.

Bellman:

In some hotels, the bellman situation is getting out of control. Sometimes, there are several bellmen: one to help your luggage out of the cab, one to bring it to the bell stand, and one to take it to your room. That's a lot of tipping. Save yourself the aggravation and buy a "Bellman Buster" — a suitcase on wheels — and wheel it to your room yourself.

Resort Fees:

Resort fees are daily charges hotels add to your bill for things you might expect to be free, like access to the fitness center or swimming pool and daily newspaper delivery. The fees can range from ten dollars a day upwards of thirty or forty dollars, impacting your bill quite a bit. You should be informed of resort fees when you check in. If you don't plan to use the facilities included in the resort fee, the best time to protest the fee is when you are checking in. Ask to speak to a manager and make your case.

If the resort fee includes tips to bell staff, you should understand that no additional tips are necessary. Pay attention when you are checking in to what you are signing; better yet, ask about a resort fee at the time you book your room at any resort.

1) _____ Telephone charges in many hotels are unreasonably high.
2) _____ When you order room service, pay close attention to the fees tacked on the bill.
3) _____ Many hotels charge for Internet access both in the rooms and in the lobby.
4) _____ According to the writer, bellman in some hotels is getting out of control.
5) _____ Resort fees are daily charges hotels add to your bill for things you might expect to be free.
6) _____ If you don't plan to use the facilities included in the resort fee, the best time to protest the fee is when you are checking out.

Word Tips

deal	交易	budget	预算
unconscionably	过度地	tack	把……固定住
steep	过高的	gratuity	小费
beware	当心	access	进入
amenity	消遣设施	craving	渴望
accordingly	相应地	buck	美元
stock	提供	luxury	奢侈品
convenience	便利	definitely	肯定地
bellman	门童	aggravation	加剧
resort	游览胜地	facility	设施
protest	反对	additional	额外的

2. Discuss: If you are charged unreasonably, what will you do?

Nowadays, traveling has been widely accepted as a way of life. And it is natural for people to expect a palatable travel experience. However, such an experience may be spoiled by unreasonable charges happening here and there. So how to deal with unreasonable charges is important to a happy and unforgettable travel experience.

Lead-in Questions:

1) Do you think it is necessary to check the bill carefully whenever you check out the hotel?

2) Do you have the experience of being unreasonably charged?

3) Will you talk in a good manner or in a temper to the receptionist?

4) If you cannot reach an agreement with the hotel staff, what will you do, keeping on arguing or settling it with wisdom? How?

5) What will you do if you still have a dispute even if you talk to the manager?

Group Work: If you are charged unreasonably, what will you do?

Step 1: Divide the class into groups.

Step 2: Ask students to discuss the above questions in detail.

Step 3: Have some groups to give their presentations in front of the class.

Story-retelling:

Listen to the funny story and retell it using your own words. You may refer to the key words or phrases given in the box.

travel	tired	continue	hotel	four hours
check out	$350	high	facilities	complain
pay	check	$100	Mercedes-Benz	

The Hotel Bill 饭店账单

A husband and wife are traveling by car from Key West to Boston. After almost 24 hours on the road, they're too tired to continue, and they decide to stop for a rest. They stop at a nice hotel and take a room, but they only plan to sleep for four hours and then get back on the road. When they check out four hours later, the desk clerk hands them a bill for $350.

The man explodes and demands to know why the charge is so high. He tells the clerk although it's a nice hotel, the rooms certainly aren't worth $350. When the clerk tells him $350 is the standard rate, the man insists on speaking to the manager. The manager appears, listens to the man, and then explains that the hotel has many facilities such as an Olympic-sized pool and a huge conference center that the man and wife could have made use of.

"But we didn't use them," the man complains.

"Well, we have them, and you could have," the manager replies.

Eventually the man gives up and agrees to pay. He writes a check and gives it to the manager. The manager is surprised when he looks at the check.

"But sir," he says, "this check is only made out for $100."

"That's right," says the man. "I charged you $250 for using my car — a Mercedes-Benz."

"But I didn't!" exclaims the manager.

"Well," the man replies, "it was here, and you could have."

Unit Four

Transportation for Travel
旅游与交通

- Chapter 7　Train and Taxi　火车与出租车
- Chapter 8　Travel by Cruise　邮轮旅行

Chapter 7
Train and Taxi
火车与出租车

This chapter introduces the topic on traveling by train and taxi. To begin with, you'll learn some useful words and phrases related to this topic. Then in Part One, you'll learn some important tourism knowledge related to this chapter. In Part Two, through watching the video, you'll learn how to take a cab in New York city (refer to Video: Cabs in New York City). In Part Three, you'll do a compound dictation: Travel by Train in the USA. Moreover, in Part Four, through listening to the dialogue, you'll learn how to ask information from a taxi driver (refer to Dialogue). Finally, in Part Five, you'll get a chance to expand your knowledge with interesting types of exercises, including readings and story-retelling (refer to Consolidation).

Useful Words and Expressions

reluctant: （不情愿的，勉强的）unwilling; disinclined
express: （迅速的）direct or fast
reserve: （预订或保留）to keep back or save for future use
compartment: （卧车包房）a private bedroom with toilet facilities
variation: （变化）the act, process, or accident of varying in condition, character, or degree
roving: （徘徊的，移动的）roaming or wandering
jaunt: （短途游览）a short journey, esp. one taken for pleasure
rugged: （高低不平的）having a roughly broken, rocky, hilly, or jagged surface
landscape: （风景）a section or expanse of rural scenery, usually extensive, that can be seen from a single viewpoint
spectacular: （壮观的）of or like a spectacle; marked by or given to an impressive, large-scale display
accessible: （可接近的）easy to approach, reach, enter, speak with, or use
prairie: （大草原）an extensive area of flat or rolling, predominantly treeless grassland, especially the large tract or plain of central North America
prospectors: （探矿者）one who explores an area for mineral deposits or oil
pull over: （路边停车）to direct one's automobile or other vehicle to the curb; move out of a line of traffic
skyscraper: （摩天大楼）a relatively tall building of many stories, esp. one for office or commercial use
decor: （装饰）style or mode of decoration, as of a room, building, or the like
hail: （招呼）to call out to in order to stop, attract attention, ask aid, etc.

Part One: Know-how for Tourism and Travel
旅游知识

Railway in the United States 美国的铁路交通

If you're tired of flying or if you are reluctant to drive for days on unfamiliar roads, a train trip may be a good choice. Train travel makes transportation an enjoyable and valuable part of your journey as opposed to a necessary displeasure; you can see miles of countryside as you gently speed towards your destination.

Long-distance travel by train is not as common in the United States as in many other parts of the world. Most train travel is in the northeast part of the country, linking Boston, New York, Philadelphia, Baltimore and Washington, D.C. Special express trains travel between New York and Washington, D.C. All seats on these trains are reserved in both coach (2nd class) and club car (1st class). Long-distance trains also serve major cities such as Atlanta, Miami, New Orleans, Chicago, Los Angeles, San Francisco and Seattle. Sleeping compartments are available on most long-distance trains and must be reserved in advance.

Most trains are operated by Amtrak, the national railroad corporation. The number for buying ticket is 800-USA-RAIL. Amtrak currently offers three variations on its U.S.A. Rail Pass, which is good for travel across the United States. The U.S.A. Rail Pass is not valid on select trains. The pass is available to both U.S. and international citizens. Amtrak also offers a California Rail Pass, which is good for seven days of economy-class travel in California over a 21-day period. You can get a sleeper car and make the train your roving hotel as you take a cross-country jaunt through some of the most beautiful, rugged landscapes in the world. Amtrak offers a number of scenic routes that will help you to slow down and get a good look at the world outside your window.

Read the passage aloud, decide whether the following statements are true or false. Write T for true and F for false.

1. _____ Long-distance travel by train is common in the United States.
2. _____ Sleeping compartments are available on most long-distance trains and must be reserved in advance.
3. _____ Amtrak is a private railroad corporation which offers the affordable price to the travellers.
4. _____ You can buy U.S.A. Rail Pass if you want to travel across the United States.
5. _____ The U.S.A. Rail Pass is only available to U.S. citizens.

Part Two: Attractive to Watch
观看学旅游

Basic information from the video

Know where you're going. Before you hail a cab, get a rough idea of how far you're going and how much it should cost. If you're not sure, ask a New Yorker.

了解前往地方的情况。打车前预算路程及费用。如果不太确定,可以向纽约当地人了解情况。

Step off the curb and face the oncoming traffic. Just don't step so far off the curb that you're standing in a lane of traffic.

面朝来车方向,站在路缘下。不要离路缘太远,站在车道旁叫车。

Hail a cab by raising your arm when you spot one with its middle roof light on.

招呼计程车。看见亮着顶灯的计程车,伸出手臂示意要车。

Avoid busy areas. Don't try to hail a cab just slightly in front of someone else with their arm out—it's rude. If you're in an area where lots of people are trying to get cabs, walk a few blocks to a less competitive location. Try hailing an off-duty cab by indicating with your fingers that you're only going a short distance, he might just take you.

避免人多的地方打车。如果附近也有人在伸手打车,切忌站在他们前面招呼计程车,这样很不礼貌。如果候车的人太多,可到人少一点的街区打车。或者向歇班回程计程车打手势示意你只是短途搭车,司机也许会顺路把你捎上。

Enter and exit on sidewalk. Play it safe by always getting in-and-out-of the cab on the same side as the sidewalk.

出入人行道。为了安全起见,务必从人行道一边的车门上下车。

Know your rights. You have the right to tell the driver which route to take. You can ask him to slow down, and you are in control of the heat, AC, and radio. If the driver says he doesn't go outside Manhattan, politely contradict him and make a note of his medallion number, so you can report him if need be.

乘客的权利。你有权选择线路,有权要求减速,有权调节车内温度、广播频道等。如果司机不愿到曼哈顿以外的地方,你可以礼貌地反驳他,记下他的工牌号,必要时可举报。

Buckle up. Better safe than sorry.

系好安全带。宁可事先谨慎有余,不要事后追悔莫及。

Watch the meter. When you hop in the cab, the fare starts at $2.50. The meter will increase 40 cents every fifth of a mile or, if you're standing still or crawling along slowly, once every minute. No extra charge for luggage. On weekdays from 4 p.m. to 8 p.m., there's an extra $1 surcharge. And every night after 8 p.m., there is a night surcharge of 50 cents.

留意里程数。计价器2.5美元起步，每0.2英里加收40美分。若乘客叫停或者超低速行驶，则按每分钟40美分计费。行李不收取额外费用。此外，星期一至星期五下午4点至8点起步价加收1美元，每晚8点后加收50美分。

Know airport fares. LaGuardia is a regular metered fare, but you're also responsible for any tolls along the way. Note that New York City cabs can drop you at Newark airport, but because it's out of state, they're not legally allowed to pick up fares.

了解去机场的乘车费。拉瓜地亚机场是标准的计程票制，但途中通行费一概由乘客支付。要注意的是，纽约出租车可以将你送到机场，却不能返程载客，因为出租车已驶出纽约市。

Pay the fare and unless you had the worst ride of your life, add a nice tip 10 to 20 percent tip is customary.

结账。如果你觉得打车还不算太糟糕的话，记得按惯例给司机10到20美分的小费。

Get a receipt. It has the taxi's medallion number on it, which will come in handy if you accidentally leave something in the cab.

索要收据。收据上有计程车编号。如果物品不慎摆在车上，收据就派上用场啦。

Video:

Cabs in New York City 纽约出租车

① Watch the short video twice, and repeat the underlined sentences by heart.

1) _____
2) _____
3) _____
4) _____
5) _____
6) _____
7) _____

② Watch the video again, and review the main contents using the headings of the text.

Part Three: Amusing to Listen
听说学旅游

Compound Dictation:

① Listen to the passage twice and fill in the blanks with the information you hear (one word for one blank).

Travel by Train in the USA 美国火车旅游

Many wonderful long-distance trains _____ in the United States, often travelling through wild, spectacular _____ not easily accessible any other way. The following are among the most highly recommended _____.

The Coast Starlight is one of Amtrak's most scenic trips for travel by train and a particular favorite with _____ people. A party _____ frequently develops, starting in the lounge car and _____ throughout the train as it journeys between Seattle and Los Angeles. You see snow-covered _____, forest valleys and long stretches of the Pacific shoreline.

The California Zephyr is one of the world's great journeys, taking two days and nights to travel by train between Chicago and San Francisco, _____ farmland, prairie, _____, rivers and the Rocky Mountains. Western pioneers came this way, as did gold prospectors, the Pony Express and the first _____ line. The Zephyr follows America's earliest transcontinental rail route for much of its 2,420-mile journey.

② Talk about travel by train in the USA with the word or words that you've filled.
1) _____
2) _____
3) _____

Part Four: Interesting to Speak
交谈学旅游

Dialogue: Travel by Taxi 搭乘出租车

① Listen to the situational dialogue carefully, and match the information in column A with that in column B.

Column A	Column B
1. destination	A. Peter's
2. traveler's requirement for the restaurant	B. subway
3. driver's recommendation for the restaurant	C. good restaurants downtown that offer meals at a reasonable price
4. driver's preference for the means of transportation	D. Broadway
5. reason not to take a bus	E. have to transfer a couple of times

2 Listen to the dialogue again, and role play it in pairs.

Lisa: Hey, taxi! Thanks for pulling over.
Driver: Where to?
Lisa: I am going to the Broadway.
Driver: Is this your first time to the city, right?
Lisa: Yeah. How did you know?
Driver: Well, I can tell tourists from far away because they walk down the street looking straight up at the skyscrapers.
Lisa: Is it that obvious?
Driver: Well. It is quite easy to tell.
Lisa: Oh, before I forget, can you recommend any good restaurants downtown that offer meals at a reasonable price?
Driver: Well, the Mexican restaurant, Peter's, is fantastic. It's not as inexpensive as other places I know, but the decor is very authentic, and the portions are larger than most places I've been to.
Lisa: Sounds great! How do I get there from the Broadway?
Driver: Well, you can catch the subway. There are buses that run that way, but you would have to transfer a couple of times. And there are taxis too, but it is not easy to hail one at rush hours.
Lisa: Okay. Thanks.

Part Five: Useful to Expand—Consolidation
巩固练习

Reading:

Interesting Things About Transport 交通工具趣闻

1. Survey: Take this fun quiz to find out some facts about transport.

1) A tunnel goes under water or through mountains. Where is the longest railway tunnel

in the world?

    A. Between Switzerland and France.

    B. Between the UK and France.

    C. In Japan.

2) The first airplane flight was made in 1903. How long was it?

    A. 12 seconds.

    B. 2 minutes and 12 seconds.

    C. 12 minutes.

3) The first bike with two wheels was invented in Germany in 1816. What was strange about the bike?

    A. You could only go in a straight line!

    B. You had to pedal the bike with your hands.

    C. It didn't have any pedals—you had to move it with your feet.

4) In 1999 Brian Jones and Bertrand Piccard flew around the world in a hot air balloon. How long did it take?

    A. 4 days, 7 hours and 22 minutes.

    B. 14 days, 19 hours and 51 minutes.

    C. 24 days, 21 hours and 8 minutes.

5) The Titanic was the biggest passenger ship in the world in 1912. It sank on its first trip. Why?

    A. There was a big storm.

    B. It hit a big piece of ice.

    C. There was a big fire.

6) The first car was made in 1908. It was very expensive. What was the first cheap car that people could buy?

    A. The Model T from Ford.

    B. The Rolls Royce.

    C. The Karl-Benz.

7) Where in the world is the highest train station?

    A. Bolivia.   B. Japan.   C. India.

8) Ellen MacArthur was the fastest woman to travel alone around the world _____ in February, 2001.

    A. in a sailing boat   B. on a tricycle   C. in a helicopter

9) In London people travel on an underground railway. What is it called?

    A. The metro.   B. The tube.   C. The line.

10) A limousine is a very long car. How long is the longest limousine in the world?

    A. 15 meters long.   B. 22.5 meters long.   C. 30.5 meters long.

Word Tips

tunnel	隧道	pedal	踩踏板
helicopter	直升机	limousine	豪华轿车

2. Discuss: What's your preference, public transportation or private cars?

There are so many means of transportation, such as bus, taxi, subway and airplane. Bus is cheap but a little slow. Airplane is fast but a little dear. It costs much money to get to the destination. Work with your partner and discuss:

Lead-in questions:

1) What forms of public transportation are there in your country?

2) How do you go to school or work? Do you walk or go by other means of transportation?

3) What are the advantages and disadvantages of using public transportation instead of taking your own car to get to school or work?

4) Do universities or companies provide their students or employees a pass for free?

5) Which do you prefer, public transportation or private cars? Give reasons.

Group Work: What's your preference, public transportation or private car?

Step 1: Divide the class into groups.

Step 2: Ask students to discuss the above questions in detail.

Step 3: Have some groups to give their presentations in front of the class.

Story-retelling:

Listen to the funny story and retell it using your own words. You may refer to the key words or phrases given in the box.

engine	break down	half power	standstill
inform	announcement	fly	

The Train Has Broken Down 火车开不动了

A large two-engine train was crossing America. After they had gone some distance, one of the engines broke down. "No problem," the engineer thought, and carried on at half power.

Farther on down the line, the other engine broke down, and the train came to a standstill.

The engineer decided he should inform the passengers about why the train had stopped, and made the following announcement:

"Ladies and gentlemen, I have some good news and some bad news. The bad news is that both engines have failed, and we will be stuck here for some time. The good news is that you decided to take the train and not fly."

Chapter 8
Travel by Cruise
邮轮旅行

This chapter introduces the topic on travel by cruise. To begin with, you'll learn some useful words and phrases related to this topic. Then in Part One, you'll learn some important tourism knowledge related to this chapter. In Part Two, through watching the video, you'll get to know various ways to save your money by cruise (refer to Video: How to Cut Down the Costs for Cruise Travel?). In Part Three, you'll do a compound dictation: The Cabins of a Liner. Moreover, in Part Four, through listening to the dialogue, you'll learn one example of a couple embarking the cruise (refer to Dialogue). Finally, in Part Five, you'll get a chance to expand your knowledge with interesting types of exercises, including readings and story-retelling (refer to Consolidation).

Useful Words and Expressions

cabin: （船舱）an apartment or room in a ship, as for passengers
cruise: （巡游）a pleasure voyage on a ship, usually with stops at various ports
all-inclusive: （费用全包的）including everything; comprehensive
fascinating: （迷人的/醉人的）having strong charm or attraction
intimate: （亲密的）close and familiar
stroll: （漫步）go for a quiet and unhurried walk
chapel: （基督教礼堂）place used for Christian worship
amenity: （便利设施/生活福利）a feature that makes a place pleasant, comfortable or easy to live in
penthouse: （楼顶房屋）apartment built on the roof of a tall building
distinction: （区别）being, keeping things different or distinct; distinguishing
debark: （登岸）disembark; put, go on shore
pier: （码头）structure of wood, iron, etc. built out into the sea as a landing-stage; similar structure for walking on for pleasure
seasickness: （晕船）nausea and dizziness, sometimes accompanied by vomiting, resulting from the rocking or swaying motion of a vessel at sea
call at: （停靠）enter a harbor
passage: （航程）a voyage by water from one point to another

Part One: Know-how for Tourism and Travel
旅游知识

Cruise Vacation 邮轮度假

Cruise vacation is one of the most pleasurable, relaxing, fantastic vacations imaginable. Nowadays more and more people take cruise vacation because cruise can help you get rid of pressures and strains of contemporary life ashore. It can also offer a means of escape from reality.

Cruise is like a self-contained floating resort that brings you to many destinations. It is a combination of adventure, excitement, romance and wonder. Once onboard, everything is taken care of. Cruising is about exploring the world. Whether you want to try new food, do something you've never done before, or see some place you've never seen before, cruising brings out the explorer in all of you. And it offers something for all ages and interests: organized activities for children, entertainment options, fitness equipment & classes, full-service spas and a variety of formal and casual dining to suit all tastes.

Compared with most land based vacations, cruising has great value and is relatively inexpensive. All-inclusive price includes: accommodations, meals, entertainment and most shipboard activities. On a cruise, you will visit a number of fascinating ports to see different sceneries and places.

Cruising is also the ideal setting for romance, intimate dinners for two, strolling the decks at sunset and dancing the night away under the stars. Many couples tend to have their wedding onboard ships. There are some cruise lines specializing in wedding on board and having a Wedding Chapel onboard the ship for receptions. Sailing the open seas would be a wonderful way to spend honeymoon!

Read the passage aloud, decide whether the following statements are true or false. Write T for true and F for false.

1. _____ People take cruise because they want to eliminate strains of contemporary life ashore.
2. _____ Cruise vacation is the most pleasurable, relaxing, fantastic vacation that you can imagine.
3. _____ Cruise only offers lots of casual dining to suit all tastes.
4. _____ Cruising is more expensive than most land based vacations.
5. _____ Not all cruise lines specialize in wedding on board.

Part Two: Attractive to Watch
观看学旅游

Brief information from the video

Research and hire travel agent. Research cruise lines to find lines going to your destination. Hire a travel agent specializing in those lines. Be sure to ask about discounts.

查询并请旅游代理。查询到目的地游轮线路，找一家邮轮专业代理。记得一定要求打折。

Buy early and buy cruise-only. Buy early in the off-season, and buy a cruise-only package without airfare since air-inclusive packages cost more.

趁早预订邮轮套餐。尽早在淡季买票。含机票的包价旅游不划算，尽量预订邮轮套餐。

Book a small cabin. There are so many activities on the ship that you will hardly use your room.

预订一个小舱位。船上会举行许多活动，你可能用不着住房间。

Be a VIP. Ask your travel agent to tell the cruise line that you are a VIP and a will-be intended frequent customer to get a free upgrade and to enjoy other special rights.

会员优待。让代理人告诉邮轮你是VIP客户，将会成为常客，以便能免费升舱和享受其他优待。

BYOB (bring your own booze). Fill plastic bottles with liquor and then use your unlimited soda sticker for mixers. Pay only a corkage fee at dinner.

自带酒水。自带塑料瓶，装满酒，随意贴上苏打水标签。就餐时只付开瓶费就行了。

Secure your own ground transport and tours. These measures will cost much less than cruise buses and tours.

自己联系岸上交通和旅游。如果这样安排的话，比邮轮安排的巴士和旅游服务划算多了。

Watch out for cash-guzzling extras, such as shipboard photos, bar purchases, and onboard art auctions.

注意额外现金消费项目。比如船上留影，酒吧以及船上拍卖艺术品等之类的消费。

Purchase next cruise. You can get a better deal as well as more credits.

预订下一次邮轮行程。订购下一次行程不仅更划算，还会增加积分。

Video:

How to Cut Down the Costs for Cruise Travel?
如何减少邮轮旅行开支？

1 Watch the short video twice, and repeat the underlined sentences by heart.

1) _____

2) _____

3) _____

4) _____

5) _____

2 Watch the video again, and review the main contents using the headings of the text.

Part Three: Amusing to Listen
听说学旅游

Compound Dictation:

1 Listen to the passage twice and fill in the blanks with the information you hear (one word for one blank).

The Cabins of a Liner 邮轮舱位

Ticket price on a cruise ship is _____ on the size, location, and amenities of your _____. It also depends on the season, with holidays and summers usually more _____. On the low-price end, cabins have few amenities, are _____ deep in the ship, and can be as small as 100 square feet. At the high end, they're more like _____ penthouses than cabins, up to thousands of square feet in size; they have great views and numerous _____ touches.

Keep in mind that, once you leave your cabin, no class _____ exist. In theory, it really does work this way most of the time. All passengers on a cruise ship are treated _____, share the same facilities, and usually eat in the same restaurants. However, some distinctions do _____. When boarding before a cruise, some Lines give higher-end occupants passes that allow them to avoid long check-in lines. Moreover, higher-end cabins usually get to leave first when _____.

2 Talk about the cabins of a liner with the word or words that you've filled.

1) _____

2) _____

3) _____

Part Four: Interesting to Speak
交谈学旅游

Dialogue: Ready for Getting Aboard the Ship 准备登船

1 Listen to the situational dialogue carefully, and match the information in column A with that in column B.

Column A	Column B
1. place for getting on the cruise	A. 19
2. time for leaving the port	B. Pier 6
3. cabin number	C. not sure
4. sailing hours	D. 2
5. numbers of ports to be called at	E. 14

2 Listen to the dialogue again, and role play it in pairs.

Tracy: Sam, where will we get on the cruise?
Sam: At Pier Six.
Tracy: That's not far from here. You told me that it would leave out at 2:00 p.m.
Sam: Yes. We have forty minutes to go. (…)
Tracy: Finally we are at Pier Six for Alaska. Let's go on board.
Sam: OK. There are many passengers on board already.
Tracy: What is our cabin number?
Sam: Cabin No. 19, Atlantic Deck.
Tracy: I hope that I won't suffer from seasickness.
Sam: I guess you'd better take some medicines before sailing.
Tracy: I will, just in case. How long does it take to our destination?
Sam: About 14 hours.
Tracy: How many ports do we call at on our passage to Alaska?
Sam: I'm not sure. Hey, Tracy, here is our cabin No. 19, Atlantic Deck.…

Part Five: Useful to Expand—Consolidation
巩固练习

Reading:

Water Excursions at Cancun 坎昆水上旅游

1. Read the passage below and decide whether the following statements are true or false. Write T for true and F for false.

Warm white sand beaches, crystal indigo seas, romantic Caribbean nights, world-class hotels, restaurants and nightlife, sounds a paradise? This is Cancun, a balmy tropical climate, water sports and a world resort where you could keep busy 24 hours a day with activities and tours available. However, the real purpose of Cancun is to provide you a tranquil retreat where you can relax to your heart's content along the peaceful shore of the Caribbean.

The original developers and the Mexican government can be proud of what they have accomplished so far. Built in 1972 in a location with lots of snakes and mosquitoes, with its government's Growth Pole Strategy and financing on the first 8 hotels building, Cancun has been carefully developed into one of the most polished resorts. The success of these first ventures attracts investors that help turn Cancun into the thriving resort community we see today. Below are major attractions of Cancun.

Beaches

The beaches with powdery, incredibly white sand and incredibly warm blue water of Caribbean Sea, are Cancun's most famous attractions. The northern side and the eastern side of the city are laced with some exotic beaches where you can relax as well as join in sporty activities.

Scuba Diving

Water sports, scuba diving and snorkeling have all become leading attractions around the resort of Cancun, along with sport fishing. Beneath the waters you'll discover a wealth of marine attractions, including beautiful coral reefs and many colorful creatures, such as dolphins. Other popular water sports include sailing, windsurfing, kayaking and even parasailing.

Dolphin Discovery

Dolphin Discovery is one of the region's most memorable attractions and located just outside of Cancun, on the nearby Isla Mujeres. You come here to swim with the dolphins, learn more about these highly intelligent creatures, or simply enjoy observing their play.

Yachting/Cruise

Various cruises are available around the Cancun coastline and offer a great way to sightsee and enjoy some truly spectacular views of the city itself, along with commentary and refreshments. Boats and yachts are available for hire at the Gran Marina de Cancun should you prefer to explore the waters at your own pace.

Interactive Aquarium Cancun

The Interactive Aquarium Cancun brings you highlights such as, large aquariums with colorful marine fish, landscaped reefs and even the occasional diver. It is possible to get up-close and personal with rays and starfish, and an unforgettable opportunity to swim and interact with friendly dolphins in an enormous pool. Moreover, you can feed the sharks from an underwater cage, visit the entertaining macaws in the bird sanctuary, enjoy a meal at the onsite restaurant, and visit the boutique gift shop, to purchase your aquarium related souvenir.

There are lots of more attractions to keep you busy.

1) _____ Cancun is an attractive tourism resort with warm white sand beaches and crystal indigo seas since it was found.
2) _____ The real purpose of Cancun is to provide you a tranquil retreat where you can relax to your heart's content.
3) _____ The northern side and the eastern side of the city are laced with some exotic beaches where you can relax but can't join in sporty activities.
4) _____ By scuba diving, you can discover a wealth of marine attractions and many colorful creatures.
5) _____ If you prefer to explore the waters at your own pace, you can hire boats and yachts.
6) _____ You can feed the shark when you swim close to it.

Word Tips

indigo	靛青色	balmy	温暖惬意的
tropical	热带的	tranquil	安宁的
venture	经营项目	thriving	扣人心弦的
scuba diving	戴水肺潜水	snorkeling	带呼吸管潜水
coral beef	珊瑚礁	windsurfing	帆板运动
kayaking	独木舟	parasailing	滑翔伞
commentary	现场解说	refreshment	食物饮料
yacht	快艇	aquarium	水族馆
ray	魟	macaw	金刚鹦鹉
sanctuary	鸟兽保护区	boutique	时装店

2. Discuss: Can we learn from Cancun and develop our tourism in certain areas, and how?

Tourism in China has greatly expanded over the last few decades. Now China has become one of the world's most-watched and hottest outbound tourist markets. Do you think that we can learn from Cancun to develop tourism in China, and how?

Lead-in Questions:

1) What is your impression on Cancun's tourism?
2) Can you list some advantages which help to boom Cancun's tourism?
3) What are the important factors for China to develop tourism?

4) Is Cancun a good example for us to follow?

5) If so, where do you think would be good places to be chosen and developed?

Group Work: Can we learn from Cancun to develop tourism in China, and how?

Step 1: Divide the class into groups.

Step 2: Ask students to discuss the above questions in detail.

Step 3: Have some groups to give their presentations in front of the class.

Story-retelling:

Listen to the funny story and retell it using your own words. You may refer to the key words or phrases given in the box.

drown	flood	ankles	fire truck	lift
save	ribs	coast guard	head	helicopter
safety	is bound to	heaven	god	

God Could Not Save Me 上帝救不了我

There was a guy named Jimmy, and his town was being drowned by a flood. When the water was around his ankles, a fire truck came by saying, "Jimmy, need a lift?" "No, no, I'm fine. God will save me." The fire truck left.

As the water reached his ribs, the coast guard came by saying, "Jimmy! Need a lift?" "No! God will save me!" The coast guard went away.

When the water had reached Jimmy's head, a helicopter flew overhead. The driver shouted, "Jimmy! C'mon, I'll take you to safety!" "That's all right! God is bound to save me now!" The helicopter flew away.

Jimmy died. When he went to heaven, Jimmy asked God, "God, why didn't you save me?" God answers, "I sent you a fire truck, a coast guard, and a helicopter, what more do you want?!"

Unit Five

Catering Service
餐饮与服务

- Chapter 9   Taking Orders 点菜
- Chapter 10   Paying the Bill 结账

Chapter 9
Taking Orders
点菜

This chapter introduces the topic on ordering a meal. To begin with, you'll learn some useful words and phrases related to this topic. Then in Part One, you'll learn some important tourism knowledge related to this chapter. In Part Two, through watching the video, you'll see how to order wine properly (refer to Video: Etiquette for Ordering Wine). In Part Three, you'll do a compound dictation: Table Etiquette. Moreover, in Part Four, through listening to the dialogue, you'll learn how to order western-style food (refer to Dialogue). Finally, in Part Five, you'll get a chance to expand your knowledge with interesting types of exercises, including readings and story-retelling (refer to Consolidation).

Useful Words and Expressions

immigrant: （移民）a person who migrates to another country, usually for permanent residence

taco: （墨西哥煎玉米卷）Mexican Cookery. an often crisply fried tortilla folded over and filled, as with seasoned chopped meat, lettuce, tomatoes, and cheese

boast: （拥有）to be proud in the possession of

savory: （风味极佳的）pleasant or agreeable in taste or smell

gourmet: （美食家）a connoisseur of fine food and drink

cutlery: （刀具）cutting instruments collectively, esp. knives for cutting food

beverage: （饮料）any potable liquid, esp. one other than water, as tea, coffee, beer, or milk

main course: （主菜）the principal dish of a meal

dessert: （甜食）cake, pie, fruit, pudding, ice cream, etc., served as the final course of a meal

clam: （蛤蜊）any of various bivalve mollusks, esp. certain edible species

chowder: （杂烩）a thick soup or stew made of clams, fish, or vegetables, with potatoes, onions, and other ingredients and seasonings

Part One: Know-how for Tourism and Travel
旅游知识

American Food 美国菜

What we eat reflects who we are—as people and as a culture. When you think about what is "American food," at first you might think the answer is easy as pie. To many people, American food means hamburgers, hot dogs, fried chicken and pizza. If you have a "sweet tooth," you might even think of apple pie or chocolate chip cookies. It's true that Americans do eat those things. But are those the only kind of food you can find in America?

Except for Thanksgiving turkey, it's hard to find a typical "American" food. The United States is a land of immigrants, so Americans eat food from many different countries. When people move to America, they bring their cooking styles with them. That's why you can find almost every kind of ethnic food in America. In some cases, Americans have adopted foods from other countries as favorites. Americans love Italian pizza, Mexican tacos and Chinese egg rolls. But the American version doesn't taste quite like the original.

As with any large country, the U.S.A. has several distinct regions. Each region boasts its own special style of food. In the South you can enjoy country-style cooking. If you journey through Louisiana, you can try some spicy Cajun cuisine. In New England you can taste sample savory seafood dishes. While traveling through the Midwest, "the breadbasket of the nation," you may enjoy delicious baked goods. In the Southwest you can try some tasty Tex-Mex treats. Then you can finish your food tour in the Pacific Northwest with some gourmet coffee.

Americans living at a fast pace often just "grab a quick bite." Fast food restaurants offer people on the run everything from fried chicken to fried rice. Microwave dinners and instant foods make cooking at home a snap. Of course, one of the most common quick American meals is sandwich. If it can fit between two slices of bread, Americans probably make a sandwich out of it. Peanut butter and jelly is an all-time American favorite.

American culture is a good illustration of the saying "you are what you eat." Americans represent a wide range of backgrounds and ways of thinking. The variety of foods in the U.S.A. reflects the diversity of personal tastes. The food may be international or regional. Sometimes it's fast, and sometimes it's not so fast. It might be junk food, or maybe it's natural food. In any case, the style is all-American.

Read the passage aloud, decide whether the following statements are true or false. Write T for true and F for false.

1. _____ Thanksgiving turkey is not a typical American food.

2. _____ You can find almost every kind of ethnic food in America.
3. _____ Americans love Chinese egg rolls because they taste exactly like the original.
4. _____ Peanut butter and jelly is an all-time American favorite.
5. _____ The variety of foods in the U.S.A. reflects the diversity of personal tastes.

Part Two: Attractive to Watch
观看学旅游

Brief information from the video

A pairing between the entree and wine. The primary purpose of ordering wine is to ensure you get a suitable pairing between your entree and the wine. Do not be afraid to ask the waiter or sommelier for advice.

葡萄酒与主菜的搭配。点葡萄酒主要是为了保证主菜和葡萄酒合理搭配。你不必拘束,大可放心地向服务员或斟酒师征求意见。

Verify the name and vintage of wine. Verify that it is in fact the wine that you order not just the name of the wine, but also the vintage. The same wine can be different prices depending on the vintage.

识别葡萄酒的品牌和年份。点葡萄酒不能只看品牌,还要看生产日期。相同的葡萄酒因年份不同而价格不同。

Look at the cork rather than smell it. Once the waiter shows you the wine and you agree that this is the wine you in fact selected. They will go ahead and uncork the wine and shoot up the cork on the table. Now, don't go and smell the cork as it's not going to give you any value, it is just going to smell like cork, but what you can do is to look at the cork and deduce whether or not the cork is tinted, or the wine maybe tinted based on cork discoloration.

看瓶塞,不要闻瓶塞。服务员把酒给你看,如果你同意,这就是你订的酒了。接着服务员为你开瓶,把瓶塞弹在桌上。这时不要去闻瓶塞,这样做没有用,因为你闻到的只不过是瓶塞味。你只需看看瓶塞,判断瓶塞是否着了色,或者葡萄酒是否因瓶塞褪色而变了色。

Taste the wine. Swirl, sniff the wine, and taste the wine. The point of tasting the wine is just to ensure that it is not spoiled or it's corked. Once you tell the waiter that yes you accept the wine, the waiter will go clockwise around the table to your party and fill each person's glass, ladies first. As the host, your glass will be topped off last.

品酒。打开瓶塞,闻酒,品酒。品酒只是为了弄清楚酒没有变质或者瓶塞是否完好。好了,一旦你告诉服务员这就是你要的酒,服务员会围绕桌子,沿顺时针方向给在座的每一位上酒,一般先给女士斟酒,最后给主人斟酒。

Video:

Etiquette for Ordering Wine 点葡萄酒的礼仪

1 Watch the short video twice, and repeat the underlined sentences by heart.

1) _____

2) _____

3) _____

4) _____

2 Watch the video again, and review the main contents using the headings of the text.

Part Three: Amusing to Listen
听说学旅游

Compound Dictation:

1 Listen to the passage twice and fill in the blanks with the information you hear (one word for one blank).

Table Etiquette 餐桌礼仪

As soon as you are seated, _____ the napkin from your place setting, unfold it, and put it in your _____. Do not shake it open. At some very formal restaurants, the waiter may do this for the diners, but it is not _____ to place your own napkin in your lap.

The napkin rests on the lap till the end of the meal. Don't clean the cutlery or _____ your face with the napkin. If you excuse yourself from the table, loosely fold the napkin and place it to the left or right of your _____. At the end of the meal, _____ the napkin semi-folded at the left side of the place setting.

Eat to your left, drink to your right. Any food dish to the left is yours, and any _____ to the right is yours. Starting with the knife, fork, or spoon that is _____ from your plate, work your way in, using one _____ for each course. The salad fork is on your outermost left, followed by your dinner fork. Your soup spoon is on your outermost right, followed by your beverage spoon, salad knife and dinner knife. Your _____ spoon and fork are above your plate or brought out with dessert. If you remember the rule to work from the outside in, you'll be fine.

2 Talk about the table etiquette with the word or words that you've filled.
1) _____
2) _____
3) _____

Part Four: Interesting to Speak
交谈学旅游

Dialogue: Taking an Order for Western Food 点西餐

1 Listen to the situational dialogue carefully and match the information in column A with that in column B.

Column A	Column B
1. main course	A. sparkling mineral water
2. salad	B. a bowl of clam chowder, a wild salmon
3. drink	C. a chocolate cake
4. dessert after meal	D. a mixed fruit salad
5. extra service	E. a bucket of ice

2 Listen to the dialogue again, and role play it in pairs.

Waiter: Good evening, sir. Here is our menu. Would you like something to drink before your order?
Tom: Yes, sparkling mineral water, please.
Waiter: No problem. Are you ready to order now, or should I come back later?
Tom: I'm ready to order now.
Waiter: What would you like?
Tom: I'd like to have a bowl of clam chowder, a wild salmon.
Waiter: Ok! Anything else?
Tom: And a mixed fruit salad please.
Waiter: How about some dessert after meal?

Tom: A chocolate cake, please.

Waiter: I guess that'll be enough.

Tom: Yes. Thank you.

Waiter: Let me repeat your order: a bowl of clam chowder, a wild salmon, a mixed salad and a chocolate cake. Is that right?

Tom: Yes. By the way, could you bring me a bucket of ice please?

Waiter: Sure, sir. I'll be right back to you with sparkling water and ice.

Part Five: Useful to Expand—Consolidation
巩固练习

Reading:

Idioms Related to Foods and Drinks 餐饮酒水相关成语

1. Survey: Take this fun quiz to find out a number of common expressions which are derived from food and drink items.

1) My brother's car is really souped up. Which sentence best describes his car?
   A. The car runs on soup instead of petrol.
   B. The car is very powerful.
   C. The car is in the garage getting fixed.
   D. It's a very old car.

2) What do we mean when we say something is a piece of cake?
   A. It is the only answer.
   B. It is only part of a problem.
   C. It is easy.
   D. It is difficult.

3) What would you call someone who spends a lot of time watching TV and eating junk food?
   A. A sofa king.   B. A couch potato.
   C. A sweet potato.   D. A suite potato.

4) My grandfather say I am the apple of his eye. What did he mean?
   A. I am his favorite grandchild.
   B. He thinks I like apples.
   C. He wants me to buy him apples.
   D. He thinks I am very sweet.

5) My friend is very energetic, she can't sit still. I could say she _____.
   A. has had too many beans
   B. has too many beans

   C. is full of beans
   D. needs more beans
  6) If I want to summarize something, which phrase can I use to begin the summary?
   A. Here's the nutcase.   B. To nut the shell.
   C. The nut of the matter is…   D. In a nutshell…

> **Word Tips**
> soup up   加大（汽车）的马力   petrol   汽油
> garage   车库; 汽车修理站   junk   无价值的东西
> energetic   精力充沛的   summarize   总结

  2. Discuss:

  "Tell me what you eat, and I'll tell you who you are," wrote renowned gastronome Jean Anthelme Brillat-Savarin in 1825. Everyone eats; but what we eat, where and how we eat, and with whom we eat: these are matters of culture.

  Lead-in questions:
  1) What elements do the Chinese and American diets have in common?
  2) What influence do the Americans have on the Chinese diet?
  3) What influence do the Chinese have on the American diet?
  4) In your opinion, who has a healthier diet, the Americans or the Chinese? Why?
  Group Work: What are similarities and differences between food in American culture and Chinese culture?
  Step 1: Divide the class into groups.
  Step 2: Ask students to discuss the above questions in detail.
  Step 3: Have some groups to give their presentation in front of the class.

Story-retelling:

  Listen to the funny story and retell it using your own words. You may refer to the key words or phrases given in the box.

dinner	waitress	notice	slide down
unconcerned	down the chair	out of sight	unruffled
pardon	husband	reply	

Pardon Me, Ma'am 对不起，夫人

  A man and a beautiful woman were having dinner in a fine restaurant. Their waitress, taking another order at a table a few paces away suddenly noticed that the man was slowly sliding down his chair and under the table, but the woman acted unconcerned. The waitress watched as the man slid all the way down his chair and out of sight under the table. Still, the woman dining across from him appeared calm and unruffled, apparently unaware that her dining companion had disappeared. After the waitress finished taking the order, she came over to the table and said to the woman, "Pardon me, ma'am, but I think your husband just slid under the table." The woman calmly looked up at her and replied firmly, "No he didn't. My husband just walked in the door."

Chapter 10
Paying the Bill
结账

This chapter introduces the topic on paying the bill in a restaurant. To begin with, you'll learn some useful words and phrases related to this topic. Then in Part One, you'll learn some important tourism knowledge related to this chapter. In Part Two, through watching the video, you'll learn proper ways to tip a waiter or waitress (refer to Video: How to Tip in a Restaurant?). In Part Three, you'll do a compound dictation: ABC about Tipping in the USA. Moreover, in Part Four, through listening to the dialogue, you'll learn a case of miscalculated bill (refer to Dialogue). Finally, in Part Five, you'll get a chance to expand your knowledge with interesting types of exercises, including readings and story-retelling (refer to Consolidation).

Useful Words and Expressions

owing to:	（因为）	because of; due to
hint:	（暗示）	to make indirect suggestion or allusion; subtly imply
intend:	（打算）	to have in mind as something to be done or brought about; plan
in addition:	（另外）	as well as; besides
thoughtful:	（周到的）	showing consideration for others; considerate
occupy:	（占有）	to be in a place
split:	（均分）	to divide between two or more persons, groups, etc.; share
pick up:	（支付）	to be prepared to pay
tab:	（账单）	a bill, esp. for a meal or drinks; the whole cost of something
embarrass:	（使尴尬）	to cause confusion and shame to; make uncomfortably self-conscious; disconcert; abash
convenience:	（方便）	the quality of being convenient; suitability
proportion:	（部分）	a portion or part in its relation to the whole
encounter:	（遇到）	to meet with
superior:	（上等的）	of higher grade or quality
profession:	（职业）	any vocation or business
porter:	（行李员）	a person hired to carry burdens or baggage, as at a railroad station or a hotel
valet:	（泊车员）	an attendant who parks cars for patrons at a hotel, restaurant, etc.
bartender:	（酒吧侍者）	a person who mixes and serves alcoholic drinks at a bar
awfully:	（相当）	very; extremely
receipt:	（收据）	a written acknowledgment of having received a specified amount of money, goods, etc.

Part One: Know-how for Tourism and Travel
旅游知识

Tips for Paying the Bill 结账小窍门

It seems rather simple and easy to pay your bill in a restaurant. You can just call the waiter and tell him that you would like to pay the bill. When he gives you the bill, you will check it carefully to see whether there are any mistakes or not and make the payment if everything is all right. And then you should put some tip on the table before leaving. The whole process can be finished in several minutes if there is no problem. However, things do not always go so smoothly. Owing to these or those problems, paying the bill can be full of troubles unless you pay attention to the following tips:

Ask for your check immediately when you finish your meal because the waiter may not notice that you are through. After all, he has to take care of several tables at the same time. Besides, he doesn't want to continuously bother you to see whether you have finished or not. But making you wait for him is also something he is unwilling to do.

When you pay in cash or by credit card, you'd better put them a little out of the check presenter, and then place it on the edge of the table so as to hint the waiter that you are ready to pay the bill.

Even though you are intended to sit there chatting with your friend for a while when you are finished, you'd better tell the waiter and pay first. For one thing, he has to wait for all of his receipts being calculated before leaving. If you are the last table he serves and you delay paying the bill, he has to wait. For another, if he wants to leave, he can go after making sure whether you need anything else and arranging for another waiter to look after you.

In addition, it's thoughtful of you to give a little more tip to the waiter if you occupy the table for a long time because he earns money only by turning the limited number of tables he serves.

When you dine with several friends, you need to let the waiter know in advance whether you are going to split the bill according to what each person orders or you are going to pick up the tab for the whole table. This may help to speed up the payment process and avoid the embarrassing situation in which everyone fights over who will pay the bill.

You can usually pay the bill in three ways: cash, check and credit card. If you pay in cash, you'd better use the smallest bills you have and let the waiter know whether you need the change or not. However, when you give tip to the waiter, you should not use many small changes. If you pay with your check, first you need to ask whether check is accepted or not. If it is accepted, you should leave your home phone number and address or any other useful information for the convenience of both sides. If you pay by credit card, it's better to give tip in cash because some restaurants will take a certain proportion of the tips paid by credit card.

Read the passage aloud, decide whether the following statements are true or false. Write T for true and F for false.

1. _____ You should ask for your check immediately when you finish your meal because the waiter may not notice that you are through.
2. _____ You should never sit there chatting with your friend when you are finished.
3. _____ You'd better give a little more tip to the waiter if you occupy the table for a long time.
4. _____ It's not necessary to tell your waiter in advance whether you will split the bill or not.
5. _____ When you give tips to the waiter or waitress, you should not use many small changes.

Part Two: Attractive to Watch
观看学旅游

Brief information from the video

Tipping is the easy way to reward a waiter who helps you to have an enjoyable meal, but rules vary depending on the situation and level of service.

服务员为你提供服务，你也享受了美食，最简单的奖赏就是付小费。小费给多少，取决于就餐情况和提供的服务水平。

Evaluate Service. When deciding how much you should leave for a tip, think about your overall enjoyment of the meal and how or if the waiting staff has contributed to it.

评估服务。小费给多少取决于吃这顿饭的总体感受，以及服务员为你愉快用餐付出的辛劳或对用餐是否有过帮助。

The average tip. 10% of the final bill is a nominal amount you should tip. This may vary depending on the quality of service and is a sliding scale from 0% to 25%.

平均小费。小费一般是最后账单的10%，这取决于服务质量，金额从零到25%不等。

When to give a big tip. There are several occasions when leaving a larger tip than 10% is appropriate and could be anything up to 40%. If the service is unusually helpful, friendly and unobtrusive, if your waiter has been particularly knowledgeable about the food and wine, if your waiter has gone out of their way to accommodate an unusual request or problem, or if you are a large group of six or over.

多给小费。很多情况下，多给10%小费也是可以的，甚至会有高达40%的情况：服务特别周到、热情友好、体贴入微，且对菜品和葡萄酒特别了解，力所能及地满足顾客不同寻常的要求或帮助解决此类问题，或者顾客是6人或6人以上就餐。

When to leave a small tip. If the waiter has done less than the bare minimum and has been generally unhelpful, also if the waiter gets the order wrong or doesn't pay attention to special requirements and food allergies, if a waiter is actually rude or abusive to a customer.

少给小费。当服务员做得不够好，未达到服务的最低要求，且对就餐没什么帮助，或点错了菜，或忽视了顾客的特殊要求，未注意客人食物过敏，或对顾客粗鲁，或辱骂顾客，可少给小费。

When to leave no tip at all. Reserve 0% tips for venues to which you never wish to return as you may find it difficult to get a table <u>once you've made known your disappointment</u>.

不给小费。如果你很难找到一个桌位，失望之情表露无疑，决定不再光顾本店，可不给小费。

Included discretionary tip. Increasingly restaurants are choosing to include a discretionary or optional charge with the final bill which can vary from about 12% to 15%. <u>If the service doesn't live up to their suggested tip</u>, then don't be embarrassed to remove it.

小费自愿。越来越多的餐馆最终账单上规定小费自愿或选择性付小费，从12%到15%不等。如果服务没有达到所建议的收费标准，可不给小费，不要为此感到难为情。

Tipping by card. This is a simple and discreet way of tipping but bear in mind that the restaurant may use that tip as a contribution to its waiting staff's wages. To ensure that the waiter actually receives all of the tip, <u>it may be best to leave it for them in cash</u>.

刷卡付小费。刷卡给小费是一种简单和可靠的支付方式，但要切记，餐馆可能用小费作为服务员工资的一部分。为了确保服务员收到全部小费，最好用现金付小费。

Tipping in cash. Once you have paid the bill, leave the desired amount on the table in a neat pile, or a bill wallet left on the table. <u>Never thrust money into the waiter's hand during the meal</u> or as you leave as it could potentially be embarrassing for the waiter. If you don't have the correct change for a tip, don't be embarrassed about asking your waiter to break a note.

现金付小费。付清账单后，把小费整齐地放在桌上，或把账单卡包放在桌上。进餐或离店时不要把钱塞到服务员手里，这会让服务员感到尴尬。如果没有零钱付小费，让服务员给你找零，不要觉得不好意思。

In a hurry. If you are in a hurry and are paying for your bill and service in cash, it is acceptable <u>to pay the waiter for the meal with enough excess to cover his tip</u> and immediately leave.

匆忙离店。如有急事想用现金付账、付服务费，可向服务员付账，但付款应包含足够的小费，然后快速离开餐馆。

Video:

How to Tip in a Restaurant? 怎样在饭店付小费？

1 Watch the short video twice, and repeat the underlined sentences by heart.

1) _____

2) _____

3) _____
4) _____
5) _____
6) _____
7) _____
8) _____
9) _____

2 Watch the video again, and review the main contents using the headings of the text.

Part Three: Amusing to Listen
听说学旅游

Compound Dictation:

1 Listen to the passage twice and fill in the blanks with the information you hear (one word for one blank).

ABC about Tipping in the USA 美国小费常识

In the United States there are a few _____ where tipping is expected. The one you will encounter most often is at restaurants. American restaurants do not add a service _____ to the bill. Therefore, it is _____ that the customer will leave a tip for the server. Common _____ is to leave a tip that is _____ to 15% of the total bill for acceptable service, and about 20% for superior service. If the service was unusually poor, then you could leave a smaller tip, about _____.

Other professions where _____ is expected include hairdressers, taxi drivers, hotel porters, parking valets, and bartenders. The _____ rule is to tip about 15% of the bill. In situations where there is no bill (as with hotel porters and parking valets), the tip may _____ from $1 to $5, depending on the _____ of establishment and on how good the service was.

2 Talk about tipping in the USA with the words that you've filled.

1) _____
2) _____
3) _____

Part Four: Interesting to Speak
交谈学旅游

Dialogue: A Miscalculated Bill 账单出错

1 Listen to the situational dialogue carefully, and match the information in column A with that in column B.

Column A	Column B
1. total of the check	A. not included
2. overcharged amount	B. cashier
3. alcohol ordered	C. $110
4. person responsible for the mistake	D. $30
5. service charge	E. whisky

2 Listen to the dialogue again, and role play it in pairs.

Mike: Waiter. May I have the check please?
Waiter: Yes, sir. It is right here. It totals $110.
Mike: Let me see. Excuse me. What's this 30 dollars for?
Waiter: It is for the shrimp combo.
Mike: But I didn't order that. I just had a steak dinner, a vegetable soup, some onion rings and a cup of whisky.
Waiter: I'm sorry, sir, just a moment. I'll check it for you. (a few minutes later)
Waiter: I'm awfully sorry. The cashier miscalculated the bill. Here is the changed bill. Could you check again?
Mike: That's all right. Does this include the service charge?
Waiter: No, sir.
Mike: Here is $100. Keep the change, please.
Waiter: Thank you, sir. Welcome to our restaurant again.
Mike: I will. Thank you. Bye-bye.
Waiter: Bye.

Part Five: Useful to Expand—Consolidation
巩固练习

Reading:

The Bill's on Who 谁来付钱

1. Read the passage below and decide whether the following statements are true or false. Write T for true and F for false.

You and your friends just enjoyed a fantastic dinner party when the bill arrives. At that moment, conversations and libations come to a sudden halt. Did someone order an awkward silence? Below are a few tips for hosts and guests to help avoid the sticky situations that can come with the check.

If you're a host:

If you're vehemently opposed to having your guests pay, then consider your budget when choosing a venue. Cooking a meal for a dinner party at your house will certainly be less expensive than footing an entire restaurant bill. Whatever venue you select, be sure to mention that the meal and drinks will be your treat so guests know what to expect.

Decide what role you'd like to play in the party. If you'd like to be the sole host, and then understand that you'll be responsible for the check at the end of the night. Adding a few co-hosts is an easy way to share the party expenses.

If you'd like your guests to chip in, let them know beforehand. There are plenty of polite, tactful ways to go about this. For example, add a gentle reminder to your invitation such as, "Separate checks will be provided." This gets the point across that everyone will pay for what they get without having to say it directly.

If you have arranged a set price with the restaurant, it is acceptable to ask guests to contribute a per-person charge. Just let them know what they'll be getting for their money. "The cost will be $35 per person, which includes drinks, appetizer, entrée, dessert, tax and tip." But be fair and honest — don't ask for more than the actual price to "pay for your efforts."

If you're a guest:

If it hasn't been addressed, feel free to ask your host if he or she is expecting guests to chip in. Asking whether or not the restaurant will accept credit cards is one way of finding out your host's intentions without looking overly concerned about money.

So the check arrives and the host decides to split the bill evenly among all the guests. This works well for simplicity's sake, but not for your budget-conscious ordering. Let your host know beforehand that you'll be ordering light (you can always say you had a big lunch if you don't want to attribute it to thrift). If the host knows, he or she can speak up on your behalf.

If you're a guest who orders a five-course meal plus cocktails, it's kind to offer to pay a little extra to cover the difference. Or if you notice a guest who is clearly getting the short end of the stick, maybe say something diplomatic like, "I don't think everyone had cocktails and desserts, so perhaps we should just pay for what we ordered."

1) _____ As a host, you should tell your guests that the meal and drinks will be your treat if you are opposed to having your guests pay.
2) _____ You should not add co-hosts to share the party expenses.
3) _____ If you wish the guests share the expense, you should let them know beforehand.
4) _____ You can ask for more than the actual price to pay for your efforts.
5) _____ If you are a guest, you'd better ask the host if he is expecting to split the bill.
6) _____ One of the ways to know the intention of the host is to ask whether the restaurant will take credit card or not.
7) _____ It has been a long practice to split the bill evenly among the guests.
8) _____ If you order more food than other guests, you'd better pay a little more to cover the difference.

Word Tips

libation	敬酒	fantastic	非常出色的
halt	停止	sticky	为难的
vehemently	激烈地	venue	举行场所
sole	唯一的	tactful	机智的
contribute	贡献	split	均分
attribute to	把……归因于	thrift	节约
diplomatic	有外交手腕的	foot the bill	付账

2. Discuss: If your friends ask you to dine out in a restaurant, who do you think should pay the bill?

While dining out is pleasant and palatable, paying the bill is always hard to deal with. Sometimes you and your friends may fight to pay the bill, which always makes a big scene and leaves all of you embarrassed. So, it is important to make clear who will pay the bill before you dine out with your friends.

Lead-in Questions:
1) If nothing is addressed, do you think the person who asks you to dine out should pay the bill?
2) Do you think boys instead of girls should pay the bill?
3) If you order less than other friends, do you think it is unfair to split the bill evenly?
4) Do you think it is polite to just pay for what you ordered?
5) What do you think about the saying "Go Dutch"?

Group Work: If your friends ask you to dine out in a restaurant, who do you think should pay the bill?
Step 1: Divide the class into groups.
Step 2: Ask students to discuss the above questions in detail.
Step 3: Have some groups to give their presentations in front of the class.

Story-retelling:

Listen to the funny story and retell it using your own words. You may refer to the key words or phrases given in the box.

beer	serve	four dollars	twenty-dollar bill
accept	ten-dollar bill	reject	single
fool	because	complain	elevator

The Bill 账单

A man walked into a bar and says, "Excuse me. I'd like a pint of beer."

The bartender serves the drink and says, "That'll be four dollars."

The customer pulls out a twenty-dollar bill and hands it to the bartender.

"Sorry, sir," the bartender says, "but I can't accept that."

The man pulls out a ten-dollar bill and the bartender rejects his money again. "What's going on here?" the man asks.

Pointing to a neon sign, the bartender explains, "This is a Singles Bar."

Unit Six

Sightseeing and Vacation
观光与度假

- Chapter 11　Sightseeing 观光旅游
- Chapter 12　Vacation 度假

Chapter 11
Sightseeing
观光旅游

    This chapter introduces the topic on the sightseeing. To begin with, you'll learn some useful words and phrases related to this topic. Then in Part One, you'll learn some important tourism knowledge related to this chapter. In Part Two, through watching the video, you'll learn an interesting outdoor activity (refer to Video: California Surfing). In Part Three, you'll do a compound dictation: An Unforgettable Trip to Niagara Falls. Moreover, in Part Four, through listening to the dialogue, you'll enjoy an interesting tour—Lake Tahoe (refer to Dialogue). Finally, in Part Five, you'll get a chance to expand your knowledge with interesting types of exercises, including readings and story-retelling (refer to Consolidation).

Useful Words and Expressions

geyser: （间歇泉）a hot spring that intermittently sends up fountain like jets of water and steam into the air

eruption: （喷出）an issuing forth suddenly and violently

weird: （奇异的）fantastic

resort: （名胜）a place to which people frequently or generally go for relaxation or pleasure, esp. one providing rest and recreation facilities for vacationers

crystal: （清澈的）resembling crystal; clear; transparent

snowmobile: （雪地汽车）called skimobile or snowcar, a motor vehicle with a revolving tread in the rear and steerable skis in the front, for traveling over snow

snowboarder: （滑雪板）a board for gliding on snow, resembling a wide ski, to which both feet are secured and that one rides in an upright position

trailer: （挂车）a vehicle attached to an automobile

helmet: （头盔）any of various forms of protective head covering worn by soldiers, firefighters, divers, cyclists, etc.

Part One: Know-how for Tourism and Travel
旅游知识

The Bus Tour 巴士观光旅游

    Without a doubt, the bus tour is one of the best ways to see the major landmarks and attractions in a city, and to feel and take in the mood and spirit of the city. The bus tours cover all the major landmarks of New York City like Times Square, Central Park, Statue of Liberty and other attractions and landmarks of the city. The Gray Line New York Sightseeing organizes a variety of tours, such as Downtown Loop, Holiday Lights Tour, The Essential New York, NYC Showbiz Insiders Tour and many others. Each of these tours explores a particular aspect of the city.

One of the most popular bus tours of New York is the All Loops Tour. The bus tour comprises of a 48-hour double-decker bus tour that includes Uptown, Downtown, Brooklyn Loops and Night Tour. The All Loop Tour features 4 double Decker buses that will let you witness Manhattan and Brooklyn along with other attractions of New York like Central Park, Lincoln Center, Times Square, Empire State Building, Brooklyn Museum, 5th & 7th Avenue boutiques, restaurants and shops and many other attractions.

If you do not have much time in your hand, the in-a-New-York-Minute Package is ideal for you. The tour comprises of Double Decker Downtown Loop, Ticket to The Empire State Building Observatory and Lady Liberty Harbor Cruise. The duration of the Downtown Loop is a little more than 2 hours and that of Lady of the Harbor Cruise is 45 minutes. The Downtown Loop will allow you to see sights of New York like Times Square, Empire State Building, Union Square shopping districts, Soho, Chinatown, Little Italy, Lower East Side, East Village, Rockefeller Center, Intrepid Sea-Air-Space Museum and more. Lady of the Harbor Cruise will take you to a 45 minutes trip around the Liberty Island that nestles the Statue of Liberty. The cruise will also let you enjoy mind boggling glimpses of Manhattan Skyline.

In any form of these bus tours, you can take advantage of sitting on top of the classic double-decker bus to enjoy an open-air tour of the enchanting city. Moreover, you can set the itinerary at your own pace. When you feel the need to hop off, do so at your whim. Hop on a Double Decker Bus when you feel you are ready to resume your intriguing tour.

Read the passage aloud, decide whether the following statements are true or false. Write T for true and F for false.

1. _____ New York Bus Tour is the best way of touring the city.
2. _____ New York Gray Line Sightseeing doesn't cover all the major landmarks in the city.
3. _____ If you are interested in seeing Manhattan and Brooklyn along with other attractions of New York in a double-decker, buses from All Loop Tour Company would be a good choice.
4. _____ Union Square is located in the Uptown area of New York City.
5. _____ You can get on and off the tour bus whenever you feel like it.

Part Two: Attractive to Watch
观看学旅游

Brief information from the video

California surfing is revered around the world, from the big waves at Mavericks, to the

rips of San Diego and smooth curls of Newport Beach.

从马维尔瑞克斯的巨浪,到圣地亚哥的激流,再到纽波特海滩平静的涟漪,加州冲浪闻名世界。

The history of surfing in California. It dates back to 1907 when Hawaiian George Freeth arrived in Redondo Beach at the invitation of railroad magnate Henry Huntington.

加州冲浪史。加州冲浪史可追溯到1907年。应铁路大亨亨利·亨廷顿邀请,乔治·弗里斯从夏威夷来到雷东多海滩冲浪。

Canine lovers and dog competition. They bring their dogs along for the ride. Every June, Loews Coronado Bay Resort in San Diego hosts its annual surfing dog competition.

爱犬人士和赛狗。人们带狗冲浪。每年6月,圣地亚哥的洛斯·科罗纳多湾度假村都会举办一年一度的狗狗冲浪比赛。

Imperial Beach. A dog-friendly stretch of sand just about 5 miles north of Mexico. It's a dog-eat-dog competition, with only the best surfers taking home the prize.

帝国海滩。墨西哥北部约5英里,有一片沙滩对狗开放。这里会举行激烈的狗赛,只有冲浪最优秀的狗才能拿回奖品。

Three categories. Under 40 pounds, over 40 pounds and tandem surfing for dogs and their owners.

三种冲浪:40磅以下、40磅以上,以及狗和主人一前一后冲浪。

Judgments for dogs. These hot dogs have three waves to impress the judges and are scored on confidence level, length of ride and, of course, a bit of moxie.

赛狗打分。动作灵巧的狗有三次冲浪比赛。赛狗在评委面前亮相,得分主要看自信程度、冲浪距离,当然还有勇敢精神。

Surfing lessons. The academy, in partnership with Loews Coronado Bay Resort, also offers surfing lessons at San Diego beaches throughout the year.

冲浪课。机构与洛斯·科罗纳多湾度假村合作,在圣地亚哥海滩全年提供冲浪课程。

Video:

California Surfing 加州冲浪

1 Watch the short video twice, and repeat the underlined sentences by heart.

1) _____

2) _____

3) _____

4) _____

5) _____
6) _____

2 Watch the video again, and review the main contents using the headings of the text.

Part Three: Amusing to Listen
听说学旅游

Compound Dictation:

1 Listen to the passage twice and fill in the blanks with the information you hear (one word for one blank).

An Unforgettable Trip to Niagara Falls 尼亚加拉瀑布难忘之旅

Hop on a commercial airliner _____ for the short flight to upstate New York, and then on to Niagara Falls by luxury motor coach! Capture _____ of the beautiful New York countryside and New York City during your short flight! The experienced guides will offer expert narration with fun facts and _____ about Niagara Falls.

Capture views of _____ Niagara Falls from both the US and Canadian sides and spend approximately 3 hours touring each side of the Falls for an approximate _____ of 6.5 hours at the Falls (time spent at the Falls varies depending on traffic, weather, etc.).

Get up close and _____ with the falls on the complimentary 30-minute Maid-of-the-Mist boat excursion (May to October). This _____ takes you to the base of the Canadian Falls, where you can feel the mighty force of the water as you get _____! You are provided a complimentary hooded raincoat to protect against the spray of the awesome falls.

2 Talk about the Niagara Falls with the word or words that you've filled.
1) _____
2) _____
3) _____

Part Four: Interesting to Speak
交谈学旅游

Dialogue: A Guided Tour—Lake Tahoe 景点导游——太浩湖

1 Listen to the situational dialogue carefully, and match the information in column A with that in column B.

Column A	Column B
1. another name for Lake Tahoe	A. skiing, snowmobiling and ice skating
2. reason for being famous	B. Squaw Valley
3. the most popular activities	C. go skiing.
4. the place for holding 1960 Winter Olympics	D. Big Sky Lake
5. the local guide's suggestion	E. beautiful crystal-clear blue water

2 Listen to the dialogue again, and role play it in pairs.

Kermit: Excuse me, what attract so many tourists to be here?

Guide: First take a look at the beautiful crystal-clear blue water. Can you believe it is 99% pure? It is also called "Big Sky Lake." Mark Twain describes it as the fairest picture the whole earth affords.

Kermit: No wonder. I can watch the bottom. Could you tell me the lake size?

Guide: Yes. The Lake is 22 miles long, 12 miles wide.

Kermit: I see. What activities can we do at present?

Guide: You have a wide choice. Back country skiing, snowmobiling and ice skating are the most popular ones. Dog sled rides are very interesting. You can go fishing or enjoy hot springs too.

Kermit: Sounds so nice. What are the famous ski resorts here?

Guide: There are many resorts. Look, the valley in front of us is one of the famous resorts. It is called Squaw Valley.

Kermit: Is it a special resort?

Guide: Yes, it is possibly the most well-known resort in California. Do you know the 1960 Winter Olympics was held at Squaw Valley? You can go to visit the former Olympic village.

Kermit: That's a good idea.

Guide: You can enjoy its huge size and massive high-speed lift system too. But now I suggest you rent a snowmobile trailer and helmets to go skiing.

Kermit: I can't wait for it. Let's go.

Part Five: Useful to Expand—Consolidation
巩固练习

Reading:

A Tour Itinerary 旅游行程

1. Read the tour itinerary below and decide whether the following statements are true or false. Write T for true and F for false.

Sequoia, Lake Tahoe, Napa 3-Day Tour

Day 1: Los Angeles — Sequoia — King Canyon National Park — Modesto

In the morning, take the route onto the 99-highway to commerce a 3-day nature journey. In the afternoon, arrive in Fresno. After lunch, proceed to Kings Canyon and Sequoia National Park. Sequoia National Park is the second-oldest national park in the United States. Big trees are the prime attractions of Sequoia National Park — many groves of the remarkable giant sequoia are found scattered along the moist, wet-facing slopes of the Sierra, Nevada Mountains, between elevations of 5,000 and 7,000 feet. And along with Kings Canyon National Park, they are both home to the giants: immense mountains, deep canyons and huge trees. From there, trails lead to the high-alpine wilderness, which makes up most of these parks.

Hotel: Clarion Inn, Modesto or similar.

Day 2: Napa Valley — Lake Tahoe

Napa Valley is home to over 200 wineries, offering world-class quality wines & incredible scenery. You will get the chance to taste some of California's finest wines at the visitor center (no winery visit). Lake Tahoe is often referred to as the perfect year round destination with terrific weather and breathtaking mountain and lake scenery. Unlike other vacation spots, you can enjoy a beautiful blue Lake Tahoe and its surrounding region in winter, spring, summer and fall. 63 streams and two hot springs feed the Lake. An average of 1,400,000 tons of water (or one-tenth of an inch) evaporates every day. The amount of water that evaporates from the surface of Lake Tahoe every year could supply a city the size of Los Angeles for 5 years.

Hotel: Grand Sierra Resort,

Day 3: Lake Tahoe — Sacramento — Los Angeles

Continue to the state capital of California, Sacramento. Peacefully located in a leafy valley of scenic rivers and canopies of trees, today's Sacramento is a cosmopolitan convergence of tall, gleaming buildings, hearty Victorians, splendid restaurants and shops. Sacramento has been called a snapshot of Wild West history in a modern, world-class city. With an excess of first-class hotel rooms and attractions, Sacramento offers an affordable and exciting vacation. Its amenities, combined with the rich history of California's Wild West, help visitors once again Discover Gold in California's Capital City.

Inclusions:
2 nights hotel accommodations;
Entrances fees to all National Parks as specified;
All domestic ground transportation via air-conditioned deluxe vehicle;
Tour guide or local tour guide;
All taxes and fees included.
Exclusions:
Air fares between your city and Los Angeles;
Laundry, valet, telephone calls, wines and liquors other than those specified;
All meals and drinks during the trip, but the tour guide will arrange for;
All other private expenses, gratitude to tour guide (Suggested: $6/day).
Pricing Policy:
BUY 2 GET 1 FREE;
Cancellation of free-fare passenger must be made at least 3 days before departure;
No-show (or late cancellation) of free passenger incurs a $85 penalty fee for the reserved bus seat.
Terms & Condition:
All purchases are subject to re-confirmation within one business day;
Standard Cancellation and Refund policy (please read before booking);
Prices may vary subject to availability/season/weekend/holiday;
We reserve right to cancel a schedule to fully refund affected customers although we will make every effort to maintain the regular operation;
We reserve the right to modify the tour arrangements for smooth operation of the tour.

1) _____ Kings Canyon National Park is full of many groves of the remarkable giant sequoia.
2) _____ Tourists will have a chance to go to winery to taste some of California's finest wines.
3) _____ A lot of streams supply Lake Tahoe with water.
4) _____ The amount of water in Lake Tahoe could supply Los Angeles for 5 years.
5) _____ Tourists sometimes can find gold in Sacramento, the state capital of California.
6) _____ It is suggested to tip the tour guide every day.

Word Tips

equoia:	红杉	grove:	树丛
canyon:	峡谷	alpine:	高山生长的
evaporate:	蒸发	canopy:	华盖
cosmopolitan:	国际性的	convergence:	会聚点
snapshot:	印象	deluxe:	豪华的

2. Discuss: Do you prefer a package tour?

When traveling, most people like to take a vacation package tour to save time and energy. Just like what some people say, "I'll pay, just take care of me," package tour is often chosen by people who wouldn't like to bother with the transportation, accommodation and so on during a trip. Do you like to have a package tour?

Lead-in Questions:

1) Can you give one example to share your experience with a package tour?
2) Are you happy to follow the professional local tour guide?
3) Do you think you have to join a package tour while traveling abroad?
4) Do you agree that package tour is an efficient way to hit all the "must-see" spots?
5) Are there any problems after taking a package tour?

Group Work: Do you prefer a package tour?

Step 1: Divide the class into groups.

Step 2: Ask students to discuss the above questions in detail.

Step 3: Have some groups to give their presentations in front of the class.

Story-retelling:

Listen to the funny story and retell it using your own words. You may refer to the key words or phrases given in the box.

Yellowstone park	kid	face-to-face	wolf
luck	alone	without a weapon	looking...straight
move back	think fast	a last resort	next cage

How Did You Get Away? 你是如何逃脱的?

A tour guide was talking with a group of school kids at Yellowstone park when one of the kids asked him if he had ever come face-to-face with a wolf.

"Yes, I came face-to-face with a wolf once. And as luck would have it, I was alone and without a weapon."

"What did you do?" the little girl asked.

"What could I do? First, I tried looking at him straight in the eyes, but he slowly came toward me. I moved back, but he kept coming nearer and nearer. I had to think fast."

"How did you get away?"

"As a last resort, I just turned around and walked quickly to the next cage."

Chapter 12
Vacation
度假

This chapter introduces the topic on the vacation. To begin with, you'll learn some useful words and phrases related to this topic. Then in Part One, you'll learn some important tourism knowledge related to this chapter. In Part Two, through watching the video, you'll see how to travel around the Universal Studio of Hollywood (refer to Video: A Travel to Universal Studio of Hollywood). In Part Three, you'll do a compound dictation: Yosemite National Park. Moreover, in Part Four, through listening to the dialogue, you'll learn about ticket-related issues when visiting an amusement park (refer to Dialogue). Finally, in Part Five, you'll get a chance to expand your knowledge with interesting types of exercises, including readings and story-retelling (refer to Consolidation).

Useful Words and Expressions

roller coaster: （过山车）a small gravity railroad, esp. in an amusement park, having a train with open cars that moves along a high, sharply winding trestle built with steep inclines that produce sudden, speedy plunges for thrill-seeking passengers

route: （路线）a particular way of direction between places

priority: （优先）something must be dealt with as soon as possible and before other less important things

convenient: （方便的）suitable for your needs and causing the least difficulty

wane: （衰退）weaken in strength or influence

stamp: （压印）to print (a design, lettering, a date, etc.) on paper, cloth or other surface

invalid: （无效的）void or lack of legal force

parade: （游行）a large public procession, often of a festival nature

preview: （预告）an opportunity to see something before it is shown to the public

distinct: （明显不同的）clearly separate and different from something else

royalty: （王室）the people who belong to the family of a king and queen

distinguish: （使显著）to provide an unusual quality which makes something noticeably different from or better than others of the same type

savor: （品味）to enjoy(food or an experience)slowly, in order to appreciate it as much as possible

tribute: （称颂）something that shows respect and admiration for someone, esp. on a formal occasion

Part One: Know-how for Tourism and Travel
旅游知识

A Money-and-Time Effective Way to Visit Amusement Parks
省钱省时玩转游乐园

For most amusement park goers, the most horrible part may not be the roller coaster but the seemingly endless waiting in front of every big attraction and pricey food and drinks. How can you get the most from your theme park visit in a money-and-time effective way?

Here is some advice that might help you. First, plan your visit ahead. Print out a direction map for the theme park. If it is a busy route, you can find another route to go to, so you can get there earlier. And unless the park is small, you shouldn't expect to see or do everything in one day, so set your priorities to save on unnecessary decision-making time. Second, buy tickets in advance, you can save up to 25% off ticket prices if you buy ahead of time and you do not have to wait on the long line before the entrance. The internet is always a good choice to find the best price. Third, arrive early. By arriving 15 minutes early, you can spare yourself nearly one hour waiting time for the most popular attractions. Think about it before you decide to drive all your way up there. When it is fast and easy, it also means about half an hour waiting time for the parking space. Thus if there is convenient public transportation, use it. Besides, for the driver, the route there is great, but after one exciting day at the amusement park, the driving may be painful on your way home. Fourth, remember that theme parks are usually spread out all over the place, and they are huge. Therefore, use a monorail or train if they are available to get around in the park. They are very helpful, especially on hot days. Fifth, bring bottled water. The prices of food and drinks in the parks are very costly, but sadly, most corporate parks do not allow outside food and drink, unless it's water. Always check its policy before visiting the park. In that case, you can save both your money and time. It is always surprising so many people are willing to line up 20 minutes just to get a hot dog in the parks.

Generally, theme parks are most crowded in the middle of the day. This is a good time to rest for a few hours — regaining your strength for another visit to the park later in the day. Leave mid-day to freshen up. When the energy of other guests wanes, go back into the park. This time, visit the attractions closer to the entrance first where it is probably less crowded now. But be sure to get your hand stamped or get some other proof of admission that will allow you to be readmitted to the park at no charge. While taking your mid-day break from the park, remember to eat outside. It is less expensive and the service is usually faster and better.

Read the passage aloud, decide whether the following statements are true or false. Write T for true and F for false.

1. _____ Getting the park map before you visit can save a lot of time.

2. _____ Public transportation is a better choice than private cars when you visit the park.
3. _____ Usually, you are not allowed to take any food or drink into those corporate amusement parks.
4. _____ During the day you cannot leave the park, then return there free of charge.
5. _____ The food outside the park is less expensive, but the service is rather poor.

Part Two: Attractive to Watch
观看学旅游

Brief information from the video

A wonderful studio tour. My favorite part of Universal Studios of Hollywood is the studio tour.
奇妙的梦幻工厂之旅。 在好莱坞环球影城中，我最喜欢的是梦幻工厂之旅。
Hollywood movie making. It's my chance to show you real Hollywood movie making at the world-famous back lot.
好莱坞电影制作。 现在，我可以向你们展示在世界著名的露天片场拍摄好莱坞电影了。
Life-like characters. There is devastation created for the site of World War II and the giant life-like character from King Kong.
人物栩栩如生。 这里有二战战场的废墟以及《金刚》中栩栩如生、体型巨大的人物角色。
Award-winning TV shows. You can experience the explosive and hard driving action of The Fast and the Furious and visit the sites of award-winning TV shows.
获奖电视节目。 你可以体验《速度与激情》飞车的爆发力，还可以去看看获奖电视剧的场景。

Video:

A Travel to Universal Studio of Hollywood 好莱坞环球电影制片公司之旅

① Watch the short video twice, and repeat the underlined sentences by heart.

1) _____

2) _____

3) _____

4) _____

② Watch the video again, and review the main contents using the headings of the text.

Part Three: Amusing to Listen
听说学旅游

Compound Dictation:

① Listen to the passage twice and fill in the blanks with the information you hear (one word for one blank).

Yosemite National Park 优山美地国家公园

Yosemite is _____ in California's Sierra Nevada Mountains. The alpine wilderness, groves of giant Sequoia trees and the spectacular valley _____ of Yosemite make it a pre-eminent natural _____. In praising the beauty of this place, the naturalist John Muir said, "No temple made with hands can _____ to Yosemite."

Yosemite was made by _____. During the last Ice Age, the granite bedrock was shaped into bare peaks, sheer _____, rounded domes and huge monoliths. The flat valley floor _____ from a large melt water lake that slowly filled with sediment. Now flowering meadows fill the valley and dramatic _____ surround it. Geological evolution is ongoing here, as lakes continue to silt up. Biological adaptation is _____ also in the Giant Sequoia trees which are resistant to fire and for whom periodic fires are, in fact, necessary to clear the dense undergrowth and make way for young sequoias. Breathtaking panoramas of rugged _____ and huge variety of plant and animal life are protected in this incomparable valley.

② Talk about the Yosemite National Park with the word or words that you've filled.
1) _____
2) _____
3) _____

Part Four: Interesting to Speak
交谈学旅游

Dialogue: Walking in the Wall Street 漫步华尔街

① Listen to the situational dialogue carefully, and match the information in column A with that in column B.

Column A	Column B
1. park location	A. expensive ticket prices
2. first trouble	B. Hong Kong
3. second trouble	C. invalid tickets
4. result	D. student discount
5. discount enjoyed	E. caught the man and got the money back

2 Listen to the dialogue again, and role play it in pairs.

David: How's your trip to Disneyland in Hong Kong?

Amy: Oh, very special. It's like on an emotional roller coaster.

David: What happened?

Amy: At first, my boyfriend and I were excited to go because we thought we'd get in with no problem. Then, when we got there, we found out the tickets were selling for a lot more than we'd planned, which almost made us leave.

David: You didn't book online? It can save you a lot.

Amy: No, we were foolish enough to forget that. But we finally managed to get a deal with someone to get two cheap tickets.

David: Good for you!

Amy: But the tickets turned out invalid. We hadn't noticed that. It was hot and we were eager to get in.

David: Oh, I'm sorry.

Amy: Don't be. The drama was that just when we were giving up all the hope, we saw the ticket man. We called the police and got our money back.

David: Lucky you!

Amy: Then, we were told we could enjoy a discount with our student cards. That's how we finally got into the park.

David: Great! Did you like it?

Amy: Loved it, especially, the cartoon character parade! It made me relive my childhood.

Part Five: Useful to Expand—Consolidation
巩固练习

Reading:

A Brief History of Disneyland 迪士尼游乐园简介

1. Read the passage below and decide whether the following statements are true or false. Write T for true and F for false.

Disneyland is an American theme Park in Anaheim, California, owned and operated by the Walt Disney Parks and Resorts division of The Walt Disney Company. It was dedicated with a press preview on July 17, 1955, and opened to the general public the following day. Disneyland holds the distinction of being the only theme park to be designed, built, opened, and operated by Walt Disney.

Currently, the park has been visited by more than 515 million guests since it opened, including presidents, royalty and other heads of state. In 1998, the theme park was re-branded "Disneyland Park" to distinguish it from the larger Disneyland Resort complex. In 2007, over 14,800,000 people visited the park making it the second most visited park in the world, behind the Magic Kingdom at Walt Disney World.

In 1955, on its open ceremony, Walt Disney said to the public, "To all who come to this happy place — welcome. Disneyland is your land. Here age relives fond memories of the past and here youth may savor the challenge and promise of the future. Disneyland is dedicated to the ideals, the dreams, and the hard facts that have created America ... with the hope that it will be a source of joy and inspiration to all the world." From then on, the dedication to all Disney magic kingdom-style parks begins with the phrase "To all who come to this happy place, welcome..." with the exception of Magic Kingdom Park in Florida. The dedication there begins with "Walt Disney World is a tribute to the philosophy and life of Walter Elias Disney..."

1) _____ Disneyland was opened to the public on July 17, 1955.
2) _____ Besides Disneyland, Walt Disney had also designed and operated other theme parks.
3) _____ A lot of celebrities have visited Disneyland since its opening.
4) _____ Disneyland was re-branded to make it sound more fantastic.
5) _____ The most visited park in the world also belongs to the Disney Company.
6) _____ The dedication to all the Disney theme parks around the world begins with what Walt said on the opening day.

Word Tips

resort	胜地	press	新闻
preview	预告	distinction	殊荣
currently	目前	royalty	皇室
savor	品尝	dedication	献词
philosophy	哲学		

2. Discuss: How much do you know about Disneyland?

Disneyland is said to be children' paradise while adults regard it as a getaway from the routine of the daily life. Work with your partner and discuss:

Lead-in Questions:

1) Have you ever been to a Disneyland Park? If not, are you interested in going? Why? Or why not?
2) Do you know after whom Disneyland was named?
3) What do you believe makes Disneyland so popular?
4) How much do you know about the story of Walt Disney?

Group Work: How much do you know about Disneyland?
Step 1: Divide the class into groups.
Step 2: Ask students to discuss the above questions in detail.
Step 3: Have some groups to give their presentations in front of the class.

Story-retelling:

Listen to the funny story and retell it using your own words. You may refer to the key words or phrases given in the box.

| ride | the roller coaster | hill | decide | get off | explain |
| impossible | shriek | | scream | realize | in the name of |

Roller Coaster 过山车

When my granddaughter Betty is about 6 years old, she goes to ride the roller coaster with her father one day. At the top of the hill she decides that she wants to get off. She turns to her dad and tells him to stop the thing and get her off. Her dad explains it is impossible. Betty shrieks all the way down the first hill while her dad explains once again that he cannot do it. Betty screams down the second hill. Going up the third hill, and the last one, Betty realizes that her father cannot stop the coaster. She shouts at the top of her lungs, "In the name of Jesus Christ get thee behind me roller coaster!"

Unit Seven

Tourism and Shopping
旅游与购物

- Chapter 13 Shopping for Souvenirs 购买纪念品
- Chapter 14 Shopping for Clothes 购买衣物

Chapter 13
Shopping for Souvenirs
购买纪念品

This chapter introduces the topic on shopping for souvenirs. To begin with, you'll learn some useful words and phrases related to this topic. Then in Part One, you'll learn some important tourism knowledge related to this chapter. In Part Two, through watching the video, you'll learn what makes a real souvenir while travelling (refer to Video: What Souvenirs Will Matt Bring Back?). In Part Three, you'll do a compound dictation: Tips for Picking up Souvenirs. Moreover, in Part Four, through listening to the dialogue, you'll learn how to buy books as souvenirs (refer to Dialogue). Finally, in Part Five, you'll get a chance to expand your knowledge with interesting types of exercises, including readings and story-retelling (refer to Consolidation).

Useful Words and Expressions

cumbersome: （笨重的）burdensome; troublesome

maple syrup: （槭树汁）a sweet sticky liquid obtained from some kinds of maple tree which is eaten especially on pancakes

taffy: （太妃糖）a chewy candy made of sugar or molasses boiled down, often with butter, nuts, etc.

flora: （植物）the plants of a particular region or period, listed by species and considered as a whole

fauna: （动物）the animals of a given region or period considered as a whole

sari: （印度妇女的莎丽服）a garment worn by Hindu women, consisting of a long piece of cotton or silk wrapped around the body with one end draped over the head or over one shoulder

bangers and mash: （香肠和土豆泥）a dish of sausages and mashed potatoes

canister: （小罐）a small box or jar, often one of a kitchen set, for holding tea, coffee, flour, and sugar

attach: （附上）to fasten or affix; join; connect

fragment: （碎片）a part broken off or detached

Part One: Know-how for Tourism and Travel
旅游知识

What to Buy as Souvenir? 买什么做旅游纪念品?

When we travel, many of us purchase souvenirs not only for ourselves, but for friends and family back home. The trick, of course, is deciding what to buy. Here are a few ideas:

Edible goods are an especially good idea when buying for a family. Individual souvenirs can become costly and cumbersome, but a bag (or basket) of local treats can be a great gift. Many areas have a specialty. If you go to Vermont, it's maple syrup. In Maine, you'll find blueberries and blueberry flavored goodies everywhere. At the shore, saltwater taffy is ever popular. Plus, you don't necessarily have to hit expensive specialty shops to find great items. Check out the local supermarkets where you'll find interesting new products for all to enjoy.

Books make great souvenirs, primarily because there's something for almost everyone. Maybe your father is a history buff, and your sister just adores ghost stories. At local bookstores you'll be sure to find just the right thing to bring home to them. Most bookstores these days have sections dedicated to local interest and include topics ranging from geology to pictorial travel books, from field guides about local flora and fauna to accounts of UFO hotspots. For the cook, pick up a cookbook filled with local recipes. Or why not consider buying books penned by local authors? They make great souvenirs for the family, with the added benefit of supporting local talent. And don't forget to check out the children's department because books make perfect gifts for kids back at home, too.

Local crafts are a good choice too. From jewelry to pottery, many regions have artistic specialties. For obvious reasons, areas beautiful enough to become favored vacation destinations often attract artists, and you'll see art studios scattered amidst other touristy destinations. Plus, many vacation destinations have wonderful arts and crafts fairs on a regular basis where you can often pick up beautifully-crafted pieces for reasonable prices.

Souvenirs don't have to be grand or expensive. Remember it's the thought that counts. Most importantly, all gifts should come from the heart. Don't buy something simply for the sake of buying. The people you're buying for are people you know and care about. Ultimately, you'll know the right souvenir to bring back to them when you see it, and that's what it counts.

Read the passage aloud, decide whether the following statements are true or false. Write T for true and F for false.

1. _____ Edible goods are not a good choice when buying souvenirs for a family according to the author.
2. _____ Books make great souvenirs, primarily because there's something for almost everyone.
3. _____ Many vacation destinations have wonderful arts and crafts fairs on a regular basis where you can often pick up beautifully-crafted pieces for reasonable prices.
4. _____ Souvenirs should be grand or expensive because they show your respect and generosity

to your friends.

5. _____ All gifts should come from the heart. Don't buy something simply for the sake of buying.

Part Two: Attractive to Watch
观看学旅游

Brief information from the video

It is a Panama hat. But actually, there is a little story behind it. Teddy Roosevelt used to wear it when he was coming during the construction of the Panama Canal. It is originally from Ecuador, but it was named Panama hat because he always wore it. It was brought in by the president. The Panama hat is for AL.

这是一顶巴拿马草帽。帽子背后还有一段小故事哩。开凿运河的时候,特迪·罗斯福曾戴着它来过。帽子原本来自厄瓜多尔,但罗斯福来运河时总是戴着它,所以被称为"巴拿马草帽"。这帽子是总统带过来的,巴拿马草帽是给外来人的。

We got Ann this basket. The best way to see what a good quality basket is by looking underneath, see, the thread is very thin, and it's very tight. So actually, you can hold liquid here. You can serve your brunch at home if you like because it won't leak, because it is so tight. These are made by the Embera women. They are the indigenous tribe that lives among Gatun. And it is all vegetable dyed. You can decide for what the wording on it means.

我们给安买这个篮子。判断一个篮子质量的好坏,最好的办法就是从底部看。瞧,线很细,且很结实。实际上,这篮子可以用来装液体。如果你喜欢的话,还可以在家用作早餐、午餐的餐具,因为它不会漏水,结实着呢!这些篮子都是伊姆贝拉妇女制作的,她们属于住在巴拿马加通的土著部落。篮子是蔬菜染色的。你可以猜出上面写的意思。

We have a special bracelet for Kitty. These are called Waca. And they are pre-Columbian art. This is the Waca for the chief.

我们给凯蒂买一个特别的手镯。这些东西叫"瓦卡",是前哥伦布时期的艺术品。这是一只"瓦卡"手镯,是为酋长设计的。

Video:

What Souvenirs Will Matt Bring Back? 马特会带回什么纪念品?

1. Watch the short video twice, and repeat the underlined sentences by heart.

1) _____

2) _____

3) _____

② Watch the video again, and review the main contents using the headings of the text.

Part Three: Amusing to Listen
听说学旅游

Compound Dictation:

① Listen to the passage twice and fill in the blanks with the information you hear (one word for one blank).

Tips for Picking up Souvenirs 选购纪念品的小窍门

What souvenirs should you buy? It depends on who you are buying for. If you are looking for a gift for a child, a _____ toy from the country you have visited would be a great souvenir. If you are buying for a _____ other, a fine piece of jewelry, coffee table book packed with photos, traditional outfit or _____ which that country is _____ for may be the best way to go. For instance, if you find yourself in India, you could buy a Sari, silver _____ or a carpet. If you find yourself in England, you could buy a tea set or a book about the _____ of bangers and mash or a framed _____ of you talking with that significant other from one of those iconic red phone booths.

If you don't have too much to think or search for the _____ gift while on your travels, then remember to _____ with foods. Sweets usually go over very well. Grab that sealed _____ of chocolate covered grub worms and you're good to go! Or it maybe a canister of Jasmine Tea on your way back to your hotel from that tea shop on that corner in Beijing.

② Talk about the tips for picking up souvenirs with the words that you've filled.

1) _____
2) _____
3) _____

Part Four: Interesting to Speak
交谈学旅游

Dialogue: Gifts for My Friends 朋友的礼物

1 Listen to the situational dialogue carefully, and match the information in column A with that in column B.

Column A	Column B
1. purpose of shopping	A. cash
2. gift receiver	B. to buy souvenirs
3. title of the book	C. *Five Themes*
4. way of payment	D. for friends
5. cost of the souvenir	E. $40

2 Listen to the dialogue again, and role play it in pairs.

Ella: Can I help you, Ms.?
Jane: I'd like to buy some gifts for my friends.
Ella: We have a wide selection of gifts. What do you prefer?
Jane: I visited the exhibition of the works of William Kentridge and was deeply attracted. Do you have his books?
Ella: Yes. How about this: *Five Themes*?
Jane: What is it about?
Ella: It mainly concerns about the artist's five themes he has been engaged in over the course of his career. Besides, there is a DVD attached to this book, which includes some fragments from significant film projects as well as commentary on his work.
Jane: Fantastic. I'll take it.
Ella: Would you like to have it wrapped?
Jane: Yes, please.
Ella: Do you want anything else?
Jane: No, thanks. How much is it?
Ella: $38.99. How would you like to pay?
Jane: I'll pay in cash. Here is $40. Keep the change please.
Ella: Thank you, goodbye.

Part Five: Useful to Expand—Consolidation
巩固练习

Reading:

Souvenirs in the USA 美国礼品

1. Survey: Take this fun quiz to find out just how much you know about souvenirs from different places in the US.

1) So I jumped into my car in my home state and headed north. In the capital, I picked up a tiny replica of the capitol building, complete with the gold dome on top, and a T-shirt that said "Welcome to the Golden State." I got some of those cool rubber raisins from the commercial too — I can even bend them into different poses! I was in _____.

  A. Florida   B. California
  C. Georgia   D. Hawaii

2) I drove through one of my favorite cities, often known as the City of Roses. I got a pretty postcard with roses on it. It was a hot day, so I took a swim in one of the public fountains downtown, then headed to Powell's Books for an Italian soda and some browsing. My friends preferred to try and find some Rogue River Ale. I was in _____.

  A. Seattle, WA   B. Portland, OR
  C. Missoula, MT   D. Boise, ID

3) Heading north from the City of Roses, I came to the original home of Starbucks Coffee. In a tawdry little souvenir shop, I picked up a statue of an elk that was made out of compressed ash from Mount Saint Helens. I was in _____.

  A. Washington   B. California
  C. Oregon   D. Idaho

4) In the tiny town of New Salem, I paused to admire the world's largest fiberglass Holstein cow. I picked up a picture postcard of "Salem Sue" to remember her by. I also visited the International Peace Garden. I was in _____.

  A. North Dakota   B. Kansas
  C. South Dakota   D. Montana

5) It wouldn't be a trip without some Mackinac Island fudge. And I desperately needed to replace my T-shirt honoring the Wolverines. So I got what I needed in _____.

  A. Michigan   B. Minnesota
  C. Wisconsin   D. Illinois

6) I had a hard time driving through the city that is said to have the worst drivers in the United States, but I absolutely had to add a plastic statue of Paul Revere to my collection. I was in _____.

    A. New York, NY   B. Detroit, MI
    C. Chicago, IL   D. Boston, MA

7) My next purchase was a plastic Uncle Sam Bank. When you put a coin in Uncle's hand, his satchel opened and he dropped it in. The money disappeared. This seemed very fitting, because I bought him in _____.

    A. Virginia   B. Kentucky
    C. Massachusetts   D. Washington D. C.

8) You know, a trip like this just isn't complete without a pecan log from Stuckey's — one of those childhood memories you always want to revisit. So I visited the site of the original Stuckey's, saw the monument there, and drove to a nearby Stuckey's to get the real thing. I also stopped by the Peach Festival so that I could get a T-shirt that read "I Visited the Peach State." I was in _____.

    A. South Carolina   B. Alabama
    C. Florida   D. Georgia

9) I stopped in what is sometimes called "Sin City" to equip my car with some fuzzy dice. I was in the state of _____.

    A. Arizona   B Texas
    C. New Mexico   D. Nevada

10) In the Sooner State, I drove to Sapulpa and visited the Frankoma pottery factory so I could round out my Wagon Wheel dinnerware collection with a prairie green casserole. I was in _____.

    A. Kansas   B. Oklahoma
    C. Kentucky   D. South Dakota

Word Tips

replica	复制品	dome	圆屋顶
raisin	葡萄干	browsing	浏览
tawdry	华而不实的	statue	雕像
elk	麋鹿	compressed	被压缩的
satchel	小的皮包	pecan	美洲山核桃
monument	纪念碑	pottery	陶器
dinnerware	整套的餐具	prairie	大草原
casserole	砂锅	sin	罪恶
fuzzy	绒毛般的	dice	骰子

2. Discuss: What's your favorite travel souvenir?

Souvenir buying, of course, is a big part of traveling: a survey by the US Travel Industry Association found that almost 63 percent of travelers said that a vacation just wasn't complete without some shopping souvenirs.

Lead-in questions:

1) What comes to your mind when you hear the word "souvenir"?
2) Does the word "souvenir" suggest something cheap or expensive?

3) Do you think luxurious and brand goods are worth the money? Is the quality so much better than non-brand goods that are half the price?

4) Is food a good souvenir?

5) What are the best souvenirs people can buy from your country?

Group Work: What's your favorite travel souvenir?

Step 1: Divide the class into groups.

Step 2: Ask students to discuss the above questions in detail.

Step 3: Have some groups to give their presentations in front of the class.

Story-retelling:

Listen to the funny story and retell it using your own words. You may refer to the key words or phrases given in the box.

muscular	department store	repeat	answer
ignore	storm off	beat up	

A Department Store 百货商店

A really huge muscular guy with a bad stutter goes to a counter in a department store and asks, "W-w-w-where's the m-m-m- dep-p-p-partment?"

The clerk behind the counter just looks at him and says nothing.

The man repeats himself, "W-w-w-where's the m-m-m-men's dep-p-p-partment?" Again, the clerk doesn't answer him.

The guy asks several more times, "W-w-w-where's the m-m-m-men's dep-p-p-partment?"

And the clerk just seems to ignore him. Finally, the guy is angry and storms off.

The customer who was waiting in line behind the guy asks the clerk, "Why wouldn't you answer that guy's question?"

The clerk answers, "D-d-d-do you th-th-th-think I w-w-w-want to get b-b-b-beat up?!"

Chapter 14
Shopping for Clothes
购买衣物

This chapter introduces the topic on shopping for clothes and shoes. To begin with, you'll learn some useful words and phrases related to this topic. Then in Part One, you'll learn some important tourism knowledge related to this chapter. In Part Two, through watching the video, you'll see how to shop for discount clothing (refer to Video: Picking up Discount Clothing). In Part Three, you'll do a compound dictation: Old-fashioned Outlet Stores. Moreover, in Part Four, through listening to the dialogue, you'll learn how to make shopping conversation with salesperson to buy shoes (refer to Dialogue). Finally, in Part Five, you'll get a chance to expand your knowledge with interesting types of exercises, including readings and story-retelling (refer to Consolidation).

Useful Words and Expressions

coupon: （优惠券）a separate certificate or ticket entitling the holder to something as a gift or discount

outlet: （直销店）a shop that is one of many owned by a particular company and that sells the goods which the company has produced

offload: （卸下）get rid of something that you do not want by giving it to someone else

fraction: （零头）a small part of something

retailer: （零售商）a person or business that sells goods to public

inventory: （存货）the amount of goods a shop has

shift: （改变）to move or change from one position or direction to another, esp. slightly

sample: （样品）a small amount of something which shows you what the rest is or should be like

second: （次货）goods below the best in quality

turtleneck: （高领衫）(of a garment, esp a sweater) having a high, circular, close-fitting collar

chinos: （丝光黄斜纹布裤）cotton trousers, often of a pale color

alter: （修改）to change slightly

steel-toed army boots: （钢钉军靴）durable boots that have a protective reinforcement in the toe

high-heels: （高跟鞋）shoes to make people look taller

Part One: Know-how for Tourism and Travel
旅游知识

Outlet Shopping 工厂直销店购物

Imagine shopping in a place where most items are 50 percent off every day of the week. As many bargain hunters know this is no dream, it's called a factory outlet.

What are factory outlets and what do they offer? Factory outlets are where big brands offload stock at a fraction of its normal value. In U.S., many states have outlet malls or factory outlets. Outlet centers, factory stores, and outlet malls all deal with major manufacturers trying to move stock. There are many reasons for this. For example, a retailer ships inventory to an outlet store because it isn't moving fast enough elsewhere or is general overstock. Companies also shift old stock to prepare for seasonal or industry changes. When retailers and manufacturers have gone out of business, they transfer inventory for resale at an outlet. Most outlets offer both normal stock and also samples and seconds. The stock is usually as good as new and retailers are required to inform you why an item is damaged. Usually, they can be products which have been slightly damaged or improperly made but are still good enough to be sold, just not at a prime retailer. Or, they are products never sold, perhaps for a reason, so rather than throwing them away; manufacturers breathe life into the products one more time through outlet sales.

With all considered, one expects to save a lot when shopping in outlets. What kind of savings can one expect? Usually consumers can get from 50 to 70 percent off most major brands. For example, a pair of Sass & Bide jeans that costs $180 is available for $49 at an outlet while Gap white cotton turtleneck, which costs $16.50 for retail, is $3.99 here; Banana Republic women's Irish linen shirt, $88 retail, $29.99 here and many Baby Gap and Gap Kids items, up to $54 for retail, only cost $5 here.

While the merchandise seems like a steal with such good prices and reasons, one has to remember that the bottom line is that companies still want to make a profit, so not everything is going to be slashed to the rock bottom price all the time. There are still stages of sales cycles to go through, even when outlet shopping. So checking out what normal retail pricing is before hitting an outlet can help you decide if one item is a real windfall or not. Additionally, if the item isn't on your "usual" shopping list, the outlet price still may not be a bargain. If you normally wouldn't pay $600 for a designer bag, buying it for that price at an outlet center, even though it says "50% off", doesn't make it a deal.

Read the passage aloud, decide whether the following statements are true or false. Write T for true and F for false.

1. _____ You can always find discount items at an outlet which offloads stock at a fraction of its normal value.
2. _____ Retailers send their goods to an outlet because they sell well at other places.
3. _____ You can find the latest fashion at outlets centers with only a fraction of its normal price.
4. _____ Even though the goods are cheaper at outlets, all of them are products with flaws.
5. _____ Everything at an outlets is a real bargain.

Part Two: Attractive to Watch
观看学旅游

Brief information from the video

Spend your money wisely. Know where to shop, and where to get the best pieces for your money. You want to spend your money wisely, but you have to know the ins and outs. So, really look at it, even though it looks like a great deal, it is not the same quality as you could get.

花钱要聪明。了解到哪儿购物，哪儿价廉物美。购物要省钱，但得知道底细。真的，看看吧，看上去这玩意儿是一笔很划算的买卖，但这种质量却是你不想要的。

The last call of department stores. The other thing that a lot of people don't consider is sales like last call at Neiman Marcus. Saks has something similar. A lot of these department stores have fabulous pieces that you can lay into your wardrobe.

百货商店清仓。还有一件事，许多人都居然不考虑像内曼·马库斯百货商店的清仓大促销。萨克斯百货商店也有类似的大促销（东西很便宜）。许多百货公司都有妙不可言的东西，可以购买放进自家的衣橱里。

Go to consignment shops. Another option is going to consignment shops. It's another tricky thing because there are a lot of different types of consignment shops. You have to go for the genre of the clothing that you like to wear.

去寄卖店。买东西还有一个选择，那就是去寄卖店。但这又是一件棘手的事，因为有很多不同类型的寄卖店，你得了解你喜欢穿的那类衣服。

Watch out for the prices. In these consignment stores, sometimes, you would be ending up paying more for an older item. So just know it.

当心价格。这些寄售店里，有时候你会花冤枉钱买一件更旧的东西。当心哦！

Pre-sell items. Also, get to know somebody at the stores that you like to shop in because they will clue you in about when the sales are going to happen and they will also pull items for you and hold them until they can ring them up and that's called pre-sell.

预售商品。你也得结识你乐意购物商店里的某些人。他们会提醒你商店什么时候降价，还会为你预留商品，把预留商品记入收款机等你买，这就是预售。

Video:

Picking up Discount Clothing 挑选折扣价衣物

1 Watch the short video twice, and repeat the underlined sentences by heart.

1) _____
   _____
2) _____
   _____
3) _____
   _____
4) _____
   _____
5) _____
   _____

2 Watch the video again, and review the main contents using the headings of the text.

Part Three: Amusing to Listen
听说学旅游

Compound Dictation:

1 Listen to the passage twice and fill in the blanks with the information you hear (one word for one blank).

Old-fashioned Outlet Stores 老式工厂直销店

When outlet stores first appeared, they were situated near their _____ plant. That is how the _____ came to be. It was an outlet for the manufacturer to sell its goods. They could cut out the _____ man and by doing so they could offer their clothing at discount prices. These prices were very close to the actual _____ price. The outlet stores would carry _____ on orders they received. They would also have garments that had minor _____ in them and therefore could not be sold in retail stores. The outlet stores didn't _____ a lot of money primarily because they were not conveniently located to the public. The public didn't want to make a trip out of their way only to find out that the items they were looking for were _____ or _____. In a lot of cases the public had to rummage through bins of clothing to make a find. These were the real _____ hunters.

2 Talk about the old-fashioned outlet stores with the words that you've filled.

1) _____
2) _____
3) _____

Part Four: Interesting to Speak
交谈学旅游

Dialogue: A Pair of Pants and a Pair of Shoes 一条裤子、一双鞋

1 Listen to the situational dialogue carefully, and match the information in column A with that in column B.

Column A	Column B
1. express excitement over certain item	A. The waist is too big.
2. talk about the size of clothes	B. They are awesome!
3. alter the size of clothes	C. We take $5 for each alteration.
4. charge for extra service	D. They are 60% off.
5. talk about discount	E. The waist needs taking in.

2 Listen to the dialogue again, and role play it in pairs.

Mary: Look at those leather pants! They are awesome!
Peter: It must feel like a rock star! Should I try them on?
Mary: Why not? The fitting room is over there.
Peter: How do I look? They're really tight.
Mary: Well, you're not ready for this kind of staff yet. Try these chinos.
Peter: The waist is too big.
Mary: You can have it altered. Excuse me? Do you make alteration here? The waist needs taking in.
Staff: Yes, but we charge $5 for each alteration.
Mary: It's fine. We'll take this pair of pants. Can we pick it up later? We need to do some other shopping.
Staff: Sure.
Peter: Mary, look at these steel-toed army boots! They're pretty heavy, but are very good for yard work. And they are 60% off!

Mary: Peter, you live in an apartment and work as a librarian. When can you wear them for your yard work?
Peter: Maybe someday, when I buy my own farm…
Mary: Then we can get your own steel-toed army boots. Excuse me? Do you have these red high-heels in size 8?
Peter: You never wear red shoes.
Mary: Who knows? Anyway, a girl can never have enough shoes.

Part Five: Useful to Expand—Consolidation
巩固练习

Reading:

How Could I Shop at an Outlet? 如何在工厂直销店里购物？

1. Read the passage below and decide whether the following statements are true or false. Write T for true and F for false.

When I get to the outlet stores, I start by looking at the clearance racks. I generally beeline for the clearance sections. I try to combine clearance products with coupons or other offers if possible. If you aren't sure when you are going, check the outlet malls manufacturer's sites, they may have specific weekends which have bigger sales and promotions. I try not to be sidetracked by "deals". I come with a list of things I'm looking for, but I won't get caught up in having to buy all of them. If there is no good deal, I go home without them.

The other thing I do is to shop with a buddy if I can. We have found that many of the promotions are so much off $100 or more, or $50 or more, but you only want to buy $25 worth. Well, if I go with someone else, we will have one person buy the lot and get the discount. We keep track in a notebook of who bought and owes what and try our best to keep it balanced throughout the day, at the end we work it out and even up. I've gotten a lot of good discounts this way.

I also don't let myself get into the name brand mindset. For me, the discount has to be good for any brand, not just because it has a fancy name brand. I might be willing to buy a fancy name brand shirt at about what I'd pay for a cheap full price shirt if the quality is significantly better, but I don't pay a ton more just because it has an expensive brand. So I rarely shop at all in the real high end clothing shops like Polo or Prada because even on sale and discounted, the clothing there is still too expensive for my preference.

Oh, don't forget to bring a calculator — sometimes the deals can be confusing to figure out how much you are really paying. One store at our trip last fall had a sale that went: Pants: 40% off, then 40% off everything in the store, then I had a coupon for 10% off one item. Much easier if you can just use a calculator.

1) _____ When you are shopping at an outlet, the clearance section should be the first choice for bargain hunt.
2) _____ You cannot use your coupons at the clearance products.
3) _____ It's a good idea to go shopping with friends because you can get more discount this way.
4) _____ Those high-end clothing shops at outlets are at the same price ranges as those cheap clothes.
5) _____ The only value of outlet shopping lies in those big brands.
6) _____ You'd know better how much discount you are given with the help of a calculator.

> **Word Tips**
> clearance products:　清仓产品　　　　　full price:　　全价
> beeline:　径直向某地走去　　　　　　　mindset:　　观念
> sidetrack:　把注意力转移到次要方面　　name brand:　名牌

2. Discuss: How to make the most out of outlet shopping?

Outlets used to be bargain hunters' paradise, with all those quality merchandise at really low prices. But now, things are changing and prices at outlets are not always that rock-bottom low, and some merchandise there are not even worth the money and time. So discretion is important when one is shopping there. Work with you partner and discuss:

Lead-in Questions:
1) Have you or any of your friends got any experience in outlets shopping?
2) What are the reasons for shopping at outlets?
3) Do you think you can save a lot at outlets, and why?
4) Do you often wear those clothes that you bought on sales at outlet stores?
5) Do you often regret about your bargain shopping? Why?

Group Work: How to make the most out of outlet shopping?
Step 1: Divide the class into groups.
Step 2: Ask students to discuss the above questions in detail.
Step 3: Have some groups to give their presentations in front of the class.

Story-retelling:

Listen to the funny story and retell it using your own words. You may refer to the key words or phrases given in the box.

convenience	shrug	rumble	chopstick
nope	mechanical pencil		stomach

Don't Have Any 什么也没有

A woman walks into a convenience store. She walks straight to the manager and asks, "Do you have any small notebooks?"

"Sorry," says the manager. "We're all out."

The woman shrugs, and asks, "Well, do you have any mechanical pencils?"

"Nope, don't have that either," says the manager.

The woman feels her stomach rumbling and asks, "Do you have plastic bags?"

The manager shrugs, "Sorry."

"Hmmph. How about chopsticks?" says the woman.

"Nope. Don't have that."

"Well," the woman says, "if you don't have anything, why don't you close the store?"

The manager shrugs, "Can't. Don't have the key."

Unit Eight

Complaints and Emergencies
投诉与应急

- Chapter 15　Complaints　投诉
- Chapter 16　Emergencies　突发事件

Chapter 15
Complaints
投诉

This chapter introduces the topic on complaining the service. To begin with, you'll learn some useful words and phrases related to this topic. Then in Part One, you'll learn some important tourism knowledge related to this chapter. In Part Two, through watching the video, you'll learn how to complain effectively in a restaurant (refer to Video: A Complaint in the Restaurant). In Part Three, you'll do a compound dictation: Who Should I Complain to? Moreover, in Part Four, through listening to the dialogue, you'll learn how to complain tactfully yet assertively (refer to Dialogue). Finally, in Part Five, you'll get a chance to expand your knowledge with interesting types of exercises, including readings and story-retelling (refer to Consolidation).

Useful Words and Expressions

bother: （烦扰）to annoy, worry or cause problems for someone
assertive: （确着无疑的）having or showing positive assurance
aggressive: （好攻击的）quarrelsome, offensive
approach: （处理）to deal with
defensive: （防御的）quick to protect oneself from criticism
hostility: （敌意）enmity; ill will
Ranch Dressing: （朗奇沙拉酱）a creamy buttermilk-based dressing with garlic and other spices and herbs
Thousand Island: （千岛沙拉酱）a seasoned salad dressing made with mayonnaise, often containing chopped pickles, chili sauce, sweet peppers, hard-boiled eggs, etc.
compensation: （补偿）something given or received as an equivalent for services, debt, loss, injury, suffering

Part One: Know-how for Tourism and Travel
旅游知识

Make a Wise and Polite Complaint 有礼有节地投诉

When dining out, we hope everything will be perfect — nice surroundings, good food and good service. Sadly, that's not always the case. The wine may be wrong, the service might be disappointing, or something else goes wrong in the restaurant. When that happens, what can you do about it?

Most people may immediately choose to complain about what's bothering them and have their voice heard. This sometimes does not work out as we expect simply because the language we choose is not right. Remember no matter how unpleasant the situation, it's best to express your complaint politely. When complaining about your issue, you should be assertive, but not aggressive. If you approach the situation with angry words, people tend to react defensively, and you're more likely to be met with hostility instead of understanding. If you approach the situation with firmness in your position while keeping yourself calm and reasonable, you'll find people are less defensive and more ready to listen and willing to solve the issue. Starting a complaint with "I'm sorry to bother you" puts the listener who may have heard many complaints that day at ease. Use this phrase if the situation isn't that serious. For example, "I'm sorry to bother you, but I wanted whole wheat bread, not muffins." Everyone would much rather be asked to do something than told. Stating your complaint as a request for help instead of a rebuke to the listener would be a shortcut to obtain what you want.

Besides speaking out how you feel, be prepared to listen. Just as you want to be heard, the person you are complaining to also has a right to be heard the same way you deserve. After you've made your position clear, step back and listen attentively to the response, even if you don't agree. It shows you to be fair and willing to work through the problem. If you approach the problem with due respect to people involved, it is more likely you will effectively be heard and have your problem solved.

Read the passage aloud, decide whether the following statements are true or false. Write T for true and F for false.

1. _____ Only when you complain with strong language will they pay attention to your complaints.
2. _____ People will be more cooperative if you complain in a polite and calm way.
3. _____ Besides being polite, it is also important to keep firm in your position.
4. _____ One fast way to solve your problem is to express your complaint as a request rather than a blame.
5. _____ When you are complaining, the shopping assistants have no right to speak how they feel.

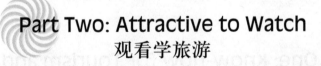

Part Two: Attractive to Watch
观看学旅游

Brief information from the video

What you need: a substandard meal, a slow or rude waiter, a little righteous indignation and a sprinkling of tact.

你需要的是：（如果要投诉的话，）一顿不合格的饭菜，一位动作迟缓或态度粗鲁的服员，这些都是你投诉的理由，但还需要正义感和愤慨，还要有一点小聪明。

Act immediately. Don't wait until you've eaten half of an inedible meal or for the bill to arrive to voice an objection.

立即做出反应。不要到饭菜吃了一半，咽不下去的时候，或者账单来了才提出反对意见。

Identify your aims. Think about what you hope to achieve by complaining.

确定目标。想一想你投诉想要得到什么。

Allergies and dislikes. It is worth telling the waiter of any allergies or aversions to particular ingredients while you're ordering.

过敏、不喜欢。点菜时，告诉服务员你食物过敏或不喜欢某些食材，这些事儿不妨给服务员讲清楚。

Contain your rage. You are less likely to get what you want by being rude or aggressive with a waiter.

制怒。如果你言行粗鲁或冒犯了服务员，你可能什么也得不到。

Be assertive. Don't be shy.

要有主张。不要羞羞答答的。

Polite behavior. If your concerns are not met with an acceptable resolution, ask politely to speak to the manager.

举止礼貌。如果你的关切没有满足，解决方案你不认可，你可以礼貌地提出见经理谈谈。

Tipping. If service has been poor, reducing the tip or not leaving one at all is acceptable. However, do remember to tip the waiter if he serves you well despite the bad food.

小费。如果服务不好，少给点小费，也可不给。如果饭菜不好，但服务态度好，记着也要给些小费。

Outside help. If after complaining to the waiter and the manager, you still feel like you have been fobbed off, it's time to take your complaints to a higher authority.

求助。如果向服务员和经理投诉后你仍然感到被欺骗、被敷衍搪塞，那就该向上级投诉了。

Illness. If once you've left a restaurant you become ill from food poisoning that can be traced back to the restaurant, you should report it to the food standards agency or department of health.

患病。离开餐馆后因食物中毒生病，而能追溯到就餐的餐馆，应当向食品标准局或卫生部门举报。

Compliment. As important as it is to complain. If something has gone wrong during a meal, it's equally important to compliment and reward good or exceptional service.

表扬。表扬与投诉对解决问题同样重要。如果就餐时出了些差错，不要批评，反倒要表扬、奖赏服务员提供的那些优质、额外的服务。

Video:

A Complaint in the Restaurant 餐厅投诉

① Watch the short video twice, and repeat the underlined sentences by heart.

1) _____
2) _____
3) _____
4) _____
5) _____
6) _____
7) _____

② Watch the video again, and review the main contents using the headings of the text.

Part Three: Amusing to Listen
听说学旅游

Compound Dictation:

① Listen to the passage twice and fill in the blanks with the information you hear (one word for one blank).

Who Should I Complain to? 我应当向谁投诉?

When you'd like to _____ a waiter in the restaurant, raise your hand, but don't wave. Most waiters are very busy but will get to you eventually. Be patient if the restaurant is _____. The waiter might have many tables to help besides yours. Never yell or _____ your fingers to get attention. Try to always remain polite. If your waiter is ignoring you, be patient, he or she may be busy and stressed out with too much work. Never _____ out or stand up at your table looking for a waiter. It is rude! Don't ask your waiter's name just so you can shout it out across the room. Don't send out family members to look for the waiter especially children. It is dangerous in a busy restaurant.

When he does come to your table, talk to your waiter with respect. Control your tone and _____, a bossy or _____ way of speaking is not needed. Remember that if the food is cool or does not taste good that the waiter is not responsible. Avoid _____ that will make your waiter want to pull out his or her hair and give you slow service. _____ the waiter as "waiter," not "sir." If you can not get any service, flag down another waiter or even a _____. If you have _____ service, complain to the restaurant manager, not to the waiter. It is more effective.

2 Talk about how to make complaints with the words that you've filled.
1) _____
2) _____
3) _____

Part Four: Interesting to Speak
交谈学旅游

Dialogue: Gifts for My Friends 送朋友的礼物

1 Listen to the situational dialogue carefully, and match the information in column A with that in column B.

Column A	Column B
1. complaint 1	A. no butter spreader
2. dressing ordered	B. overdone chicken
3. complaint 2	C. wrong salad dressing
4. complaint 3	D. Thousand Island
5. compensation	E. 50% off

2 Listen to the dialogue again, and role play it in pairs.

Peter: Excuse me, miss?
Waitress: Yes, sir. What can I do for you?
Peter: I'm afraid they have put the wrong dressing on my salad. This is Ranch Dressing, and I want Thousand Island.
Waitress: Oh, I'm awfully sorry. I'll get you another one.
Peter: Thank you. And can you get me a butter spreader? I don't have one here. And my

finger is not that clean.

Waitress: Sure! I'm so sorry, sir. Sometimes when we are in a hurry, we might make such mistakes. I'd be back with it right now.

Peter: Thanks! Listen, I really hate to bother you more, but my chicken is too tough. I tried but I really cannot take this.

Waitress: Oh, I'm terribly sorry, sir. I'll send it back to the kitchen. I can bring you something else, if you'd like.

Peter: Thank you. I think I'm done here. Can I have my bill?

Waitress: Sure, sir. We're so sorry about what happened. And we'll offer you a 50% discount as compensation. Hope to see you again.

Peter: Well, we'll see.

Part Five: Useful to Expand—Consolidation
巩固练习

Reading:

Customer Service 客户服务

1. Survey: Take this fun quiz to find out if you can offer good services.

1) You should greet and say the company's name when you answer the phone.
   ○ True   ○ False

2) Your clothes matter when dealing face to face with customers.
   ○ True   ○ False

3) You should tell the customer if he/she is at fault.
   ○ True   ○ False

4) Argue with the customer. Stand for your right.
   ○ True   ○ False

5) Apologize to the customer even if the fault was done by another staff.
   ○ True   ○ False

6) When shaking hands, your hand should go soft and let the other party squeeze it.
   ○ True   ○ False

7) Feedback by clients or customers is not important.
   ○ True   ○ False

8) We must put ourselves in the customers' shoes if they lodge a complaint.
   ○ True   ○ False

9) Repeat customers' complaint after they have said it to be sure.
   ○ True   ○ False

10) Give away name cards with only one hand.
    ○ True   ○ False

Word Tips

greet	迎接	matter	要紧
fault	过错	apologize	道歉
shake	摇动	squeeze	用力挤压
feedback	回馈	lodge	正式提出

2. Discuss: Can you make a good service person?

As a service person, one might be dealing with 10 customers or 200 customers a day. Whether the interaction between you and your customer is a positive or negative one largely depends on the way you react to their demand or complaint. Work with your partner and discuss:

Lead-in Questions:

1) Have you ever thought of working as a waiter or waitress? If not, why?

2) As a restaurant manager, how would you feel about the people who complain a lot?

3) As a waiter or waitress, do you believe it is acceptable to stand up for one's right when the customer demands unreasonably?

4) Do you think it is acceptable for a waiter or waitress to swear back if his or her customer swears first?

5) Do you believe the customer has the right to refuse to pay the bill if he is not happy with the service?

Group Work: Can you make a good service person?

Step 1: Divide the class into groups.

Step 2: Ask students to discuss the above questions in detail.

Step 3: Have some groups to give their presentations in front of the class.

Story-retelling:

Listen to the funny story and retell it using your own words. You may refer to the key words or phrases given in the box.

customer	bother	waiter	restaurant
air conditioner	turn up	turn down	surprisingly
angry	pest		

I Don't Care 我无所谓

A customer was bothering the waiter in a restaurant. First, he asked that the air conditioning be turned up because he was too hot, then he asked it be turned down because he was too cold, and so on for about half an hour.

Surprisingly, the waiter was very patient; he walked back and forth and never once got angry. So finally, a second customer asked him why he didn't throw out the pest.

"Oh I don't care," said the waiter with a smile. "We don't even have an air conditioner."

Chapter 16
Emergencies
突发事件

This chapter introduces the topic on problems and emergencies. To begin with, you'll learn some useful words and phrases related to this topic. Then in Part One, you'll learn some important tourism knowledge related to this chapter. In Part Two, through watching the video, you'll learn how to prepare for a safe travel (refer to Video: Tips for Travelers' Security). In Part Three, you'll do a compound dictation: Medicines for Travel. Moreover, in Part Four, through listening to the dialogue, you'll learn what to do after a car incident (refer to Dialogue). Finally, in Part Five, you'll get a chance to expand your knowledge with interesting types of exercises, including readings and story-retelling (refer to Consolidation).

Useful Words and Expressions

hazard: （危险）something causing unavoidable danger, peril, risk, or difficulty
seismic: （地震的）pertaining to, of the nature of, or caused by an earthquake or vibration of the earth, whether due to natural or artificial causes.
endemic: （地方的）belonging exclusively or confined to a particular place
instability: （不稳定）the quality or state of being unstable; lack of stability or firmness
inbound: （归本国的）inward bound
prescription: （处方）a direction, usually written, by the physician to the pharmacist for the preparation and use of a medicine or remedy
refill: （替换物）a material, supply, or the like, to replace something that has been used up
laxative: （通便的药）a medicine or agent for relieving constipation
diarrhea: （腹泻）an intestinal disorder characterized by abnormal frequency and fluidity of fecal evacuations
rehydration: （补液）the restoration of fluid to a dehydrated substance
dehydration: （脱水）an abnormal loss of water from the body, esp. from illness or physical exertion
gauze: （纱布）a surgical dressing of loosely woven cotton
antiseptic: （消毒剂）a substance that inhibits the proliferation of infectious agents
repellent: （防虫剂）something that repels, as a substance that keeps away insects
bumper: （保险杠）a metal guard, usually horizontal, for protecting the front or rear of an automobile, truck, etc.

Part One: Know-how for Tourism and Travel
旅游知识

Travel Safety 旅游安全

While most trips will be pleasant and without incident, it is a good idea to do some research and be prepared before you leave home. Be attentive to basic preparations (such as copying essential documentation and noting emergency contact information) and ensure that you are aware of any risk of seasonal natural hazards, seismic activity, extreme weather patterns, disease outbreaks or endemic health issues, personal security concerns, or any patterns of socio-political instability in your destination. One good place to start your research is with the websites of government agencies that report safety, security and health issues related to travel in a foreign country.

Just as we travel to places with different climates and customs, we also travel to locations faced with different types of hazards that could interrupt trip plans or have a potential impact on our health and security. Consequently, it is as important to familiarize ourselves with basic knowledge about cultural norms in a country as it is to be aware of any risks we may encounter while travelling. There are many sources that can prepare travelers for potential crisis event in a destination. Websites, such as news and weather sites and your country's foreign office website are good places to start.

If an event hits before you leave for your destination, there could be cancellation or postponement of inbound tourism. Check on the status of the event and if required, find out what procedures may be in place for altering your schedule.

Read the passage aloud, decide whether the following statements are true or false. Write T for true and F for false.

1. _____ Basic preparations include copying essential documentation and noting emergency contact information.
2. _____ You should try to find out whether there are any patterns of socio-political instability in your destination.
3. _____ The website of government agencies is a good place to find information about safety, security, and health issues related to travel in a foreign country.
4. _____ We do not have to get basic knowledge about cultural norms in the destination country.
5. _____ If an event hits before you leave for your destination, you have to cancel your trip.

Part Two: Attractive to Watch
观看学旅游

Brief information from the video

Get ready before you travel. We are going to talk about security. When you travel in other parts of the world, it is very important to find out the US embassy in terms of the local area because if you ever need anything, it is better to know where it is before you need it.

旅行前做好准备。我们要讨论安全问题。前往世界上其他地方旅行，查询美国大使馆所在国家的位置很重要。如果需要，最好行前搞清楚。

Keep a copy of your passport. You need a copy of your passport. The reason you need it is because if someone takes your passport, you are not going to be able to identify yourself to the US embassy. Leave one copy of this page at home; one copy with you and keep it somewhere else other than where your passport is.

保留一份护照复印件。你得复印一份护照，因为如果有人拿走你的护照，你就无法向美国大使馆证明你的身份。把这一份复印件留在家里，另一份带走，但不要与随身携带的护照放在一起。

Find out the US embassy abroad. Find out where the US embassy is before leaving the United States. It will give you a list of the US embassy locations in all parts of the world. If you have to find out the extra information ahead of time, it is good for you because that is the way you want it. But if you do need it, you are prepared. Make sure you are secure. And that starts with information.

查询美国驻外大使馆。离美前，查询美国大使馆所在国家的地点。大使馆会给你提供一份清单，上面有美国大使馆在世界各地的位置。如果你事先还想知道其他信息，清单会对你有帮助，你可查到想要的信息。如果你的确需要这份清单，那你得准备好。确保旅行安全，从寻找信息开始。

Video:

Tips for Travelers' Security 旅游安全小知识

1 Watch the short video twice, and repeat the underlined sentences by heart.

1) _____

2) _____

3) _____

2 Watch the video again, and review the main contents using the headings of the text.

Part Three: Amusing to Listen
听说学旅游

Compound Dictation:

1) Listen to the passage twice and fill in the blanks with the information you hear (one word for one blank).

Medicines for Travel 旅游必备药品

Nothing can ruin a vacation faster than an unexpected _____ or injury. So before taking your next trip, be sure to _____ a small kit of emergency supplies and medications in case the unexpected happens.

The most important items to remember to bring with you on any trip are an ample supply of your _____ medications. With a good supply in hand, you won't have to worry about getting a _____ if your luggage is lost or there's a _____ in your returning flight.

_____ on how your body usually reacts when you're away from your home routines, you might want to bring along some antacids, a laxative, and/or anti-diarrheal medication. If you are traveling to an area where traveler's diarrhea is common, consider packing oral rehydration salts. Drinking these salts mixed with clean, bottled water can help offset dehydration _____ by severe diarrhea.

Take along such _____ emergency supplies as bandages, gauze and tape, eye drops, and antiseptic wipes. If you're embarking on a more active vacation, an elastic support bandage might come in handy for an unexpected strain or sprain.

Don't forget insect repellent and plenty of sunscreen. Though you probably won't use a vast _____ of your emergency supplies during travel, chances are at least an item or two will turn out to be _____. And that in itself makes it worth the space in your luggage.

2) Talk about the medicines for travel with the words that you've filled.

1) _____
2) _____
3) _____

Part Four: Interesting to Speak
交谈学旅游

Dialogue: A Car Accident 车祸事故

1 Listen to the situational dialogue carefully, and match the information in column A with that in column B.

Column A	Column B
1. person causing the car accident	A. insurance number and ID
2. damaged part of Sue's car	B. Jim
3. cause of the accident	C. bumper
4. reason for Sue to call the police	D. Jim's suddenly changing the lane without giving signals and overtaking Sue's car
5. items Jim shows to Sue	E. Jim denies it is his fault

2 Listen to the dialogue again, and role play it in pairs.

Sue: Why did you run into me?
Jim: I didn't mean to. It was an accident.
Sue: You have completely damaged my car.
Jim: I did not. It looks perfectly fine.
Sue: You don't see what happened to my bumper?
Jim: What did I do to it?
Sue: You smashed my bumper in with your car.
Jim: But this is not my fault.
Sue: You suddenly changed the lane without giving signals and tried to overtake me.
Jim: It is you who did the dangerous thing.
Sue: In this case, I'll call the police.
Jim: Stop doing it. Let me give you my car insurance number and show you my ID. I'll call to report this accident. My insurance company will take care of it shortly.

Part Five: Useful to Expand—Consolidation
巩固练习

Reading:

Emergencies 应急知识

1. Survey: How much do you know about emergency preparedness? In a crisis, would you panic?

The answer may surprise you. Take this fun quiz to test your knowledge on various disasters and emergency preparedness items.

1) As long as a thunderstorm is five miles away or farther from you, you are pretty safe from lightning strikes.

    A. True   B. False

2) When an earthquake strikes, you should _____.

    A. run outside to avoid falling building debris

    B. take cover under a heavy piece of furniture

    C. panic

    D. lean against an inside wall or stand under an inside doorway

    E. B and/or D

3) Which areas of the United States are vulnerable to earthquakes?

    A. The West Coast, particularly California.

    B. The Eastern Seaboard.

    C. The central United States.

    D. All 50 states.

4) What's the most common disaster that occurs in the United States?

    A. Fire.   B. Flood.

    C. Earthquake.   D. Tornado.

5) What's the number one disaster related killer in the United States?

    A. Fire.   B. Flood.

    C. Earthquake.   D. Tornado.

6) If your car stalls while you're evacuating from a flood, you should _____.

    A. stay inside the car until assistance can arrive

    B. leave it

    C. call a towing service

    D. flag someone down to help you start it

7) When treating frostbite, you should _____.

    A. rub the limbs down with snow

    B. give the victim a cup of hot chocolate to warm up

    C. gradually warm the body by wrapping in dry blankets

    D. plunge the affected areas in HOT water

8) The most dangerous part of a hurricane is _____.

    A. the breaking waves   B. the gale-force winds

    C. the flood-causing rains   D. the landslides

Word Tips

lightning	闪电	debris	散落的碎片
vulnerable	易受伤害的	tornado	龙卷风
evacuate	撤离	tow	拖；拉
frostbite	冻伤	plunge	投入
hurricane	飓风	gale-force	强风的
landslide	山崩		

2. Discuss: What items should be put in your travel emergency kit?

If you're planning an international trip, especially to a destination that's an undeveloped country, keeping a travel emergency kit can be a lifesaver.

Lead-in Questions:

1) Did you have any emergency when you traveled?
2) How did you solve it with your prepared emergency kit?
3) Do you think it is necessary to have a travel emergency kit for international travel?
4) What factors should be taken into consideration when you prepare a travel emergency kit?

Group Work: What items should be put in your travel emergency kit?

Step 1: Divide the class into groups.
Step 2: Ask students to discuss the above questions in detail.
Step 3: Have some groups to give their presentations in front of the class.

Story-retelling:

Listen to the funny story and retell it using your own words. You may refer to the key words or phrases given in the box.

| fall to the ground | roll back | cell phone | emergency services |
| operator | take it easy | make sure | a shot |

Let's Make Sure He's Dead 确认他已死亡

A couple of hunters are out in the woods when one of them falls to the ground. He doesn't seem to be breathing; his eyes are rolled back in his head. The other hunter whips out his cell phone and calls the emergency services. He gasps to the operator, "My friend is dead! What can I do?" The operator, in a calm soothing voice, says, "Just take it easy. I can help. First, let's make sure he's dead." There is a silence, and then a shot is heard. The hunter's voice comes back on the line. He says, "OK, now what?"

《旅游英语视听说(第二版)》

尊敬的老师：

　　您好！

　　为了方便您更好地使用本教材，获得最佳教学效果，我们特向使用该书作为教材的教师赠送本教材配套参考资料。如有需要，请完整填写"教师联系表"并加盖所在单位系（院）公章，免费向出版社索取。

　　本教材听力录音可至www.pup.cn免费下载，也可向授课老师赠送听力录音的光盘版。

北京大学出版社

教 师 联 系 表

教材名称	《旅游英语视听说（第二版）》					
姓名：		性别：		职务：		职称：
E-mail：		联系电话：		邮政编码：		
供职学校：			所在院系：			（章）
学校地址：						
教学科目与年级：			班级人数：			
通信地址：						

　　填写完毕后，请将此表邮寄给我们，我们将为您免费寄送本教材配套资料，谢谢！

北京市海淀区成府路205号
北京大学出版社外语编辑部　李　颖　　邮　购　部　电　话：010-62534449
邮政编码：100871　　　　　　　　　　　市场营销部电话：010-62750672
电子邮箱：evalee1770@sina.com　　　　　外语编辑部电话：010-62754382